The Joy of the Saints

To my sister Joan

affectionately and gratefully

and for a week's retreat

in her Dorset home

enabling me to write

the introductory essay

The Joy of the Saints

Spiritual Readings throughout the Year

INTRODUCED AND ARRANGED BY

ROBERT LLEWELYN

Illustrated by Sister Elizabeth Ruth ODC

TEMPLEGATE PUBLISHERS
Springfield, Illinois

First published in 1988 by
Darton, Longman and Todd Ltd
1 Spencer Court
140-142 Wandsworth High St
London SW18 4JJ

First published in 1989 in the United States by
Templegate Publishers
302 East Adams Street
Springfield, Illinois 62701

All royalties earned by the sale of this book are being given to
The Julian Shrine, c/o All Hallows
Rouen Road, Norwich

ISBN 0-87243-191-6

Contents

NOTE: In the United States the
'Enfolded in Love' series is known as
the 'Daily Readings' series.

Preface

On 8 May 1980, to mark the inclusion of Julian of Norwich in the new Church of England Calendar, Messrs Darton, Longman and Todd published a book of daily readings from Julian, produced by members of her Shrine in Norwich. *Enfolded in Love* rapidly became a best-seller and after seven years is still being discovered. Three years later the book was followed by *The Dart of Longing Love*, being daily readings from *The Cloud of Unknowing* which was written by an unknown author contemporary with Julian. Gradually a series evolved and at the time of publication there are seventeen books available, each containing sixty 'daily readings' divided into short paragraphs for meditation or simpler reading. The publishers have now asked me to prepare a book for use throughout the year, drawing on the readings of what has now come to be known as the 'Enfolded in Love' series.

In undertaking this task I have had to decide what plan should be adopted in making and arranging the selections. Selections might, for example, have been arranged by themes, but I have decided against that as the book is primarily intended for daily readings, and it makes little sense to offer, for example, faith or love or prayer for January, and not to return to the subject until the following year. Hence the arrangement will be found to be somewhat random (though the immoveable feasts of the Church have been observed within the limits made possible by the source material), excepting that every now and again consecutive readings are taken from the same source book when they relate closely with one another. It will also be found that where the source book develops a theme making the order of readings important – *The Dart of Longing Love* and *Lamps of Fire* are cases in point – the order has been kept, so that the reader can, by reference to the index, follow the theme throughout the book. I had at one time wondered whether to include *The Dart of Longing Love* in these selections, since it offers a different style of reading from the others, but the book, after four years, remains one of the best-sellers in the series, and it is likely that there will be readers of this present book who will be glad to be introduced to it. Let me, however, sound a note of warning. If the reader wishes to pursue the 'work' (the author's name for his way of prayer) of *The Cloud of Unknowing*, he or she should obtain either the full edition of *The Cloud*, or at least of *The Dart*, as nothing more than an outline sketch can be given here. The readings are there to whet the appetites of those who may be drawn to this 'work', though, as will be seen, some readings are of a general nature.

A book of this sort may be expected to be used in a variety of ways. Some may wish to use the readings as a basis for their daily meditations. For the most part they speak to the heart, and can be expected to make their impression, even though later we may have little or no recollection of what has been read. This is unimportant, as unimportant as being able to remember what we ate at our last meal. The meal made its impact at the time and will continue to sustain us until we eat again. It will be the same with our time of prayer. It is the seeking of God which matters and not any explanation we can later give. As for the finding, the time and manner rests with him. So long as our prayer time is marked by an overall desire for God, confused and inarticulate it may be, all is well. Not every reading, however – for example, some of those from *The Dart of Longing Love* – lends itself to be taken in this way. They need to be read in the first place more with the mind than the heart, though in the application of the 'work' of *The Dart* it is the heart and will which are at work. As the writer puts it: 'By love he may be grasped and held; by thought never.'

December 1987   ROBERT LLEWELYN
The Julian Shrine
c/o All Hallows
Rouen Road
Norwich

NOTE

I am most grateful to the editors of the volumes in the 'Enfolded in Love' series for kindly allowing me to draw upon their selections. I am also grateful to copyright holders for permission to use material quoted on the following pages (details of sources are given in the relevant books in the series): Banner of Truth Trust 170; Cambridge University Press 161, 286; Dr J. P. Clancy 61, 360; Collins 120; Constable 63, 208, 347; Mowbrays 42, 65 para. 2, 104 paras. 2 and 3, 136; Oxford University Press 77, 213, 262 and all readings from *The Mirror of Love*; Paulist Press 42 para. 2; A. D. Peters 174; Routledge and Kegan Paul 363; SLG Press 65 para. 1, 247, 332 para. 2; University of Wales Press 91, 181.

The Joy of the Saints

The nature of the way

In the reading on page 298 of this book, William Law tells how Jacob Boehme, the German mystic, 'absolutely requires his reader to be in the way of the returning prodigal'. This striking and, perhaps, to some, unexpected observation may serve to introduce us to the lives of the saints. 'It is not rules of morality observed, or an outward blameless form of life that will do,' continues Law, 'for pride, vanity, envy, self-love and love of the world can be and often are the heart of such a morality of life. But the state of the lost son is quite another thing.' The returning prodigal must necessarily be caught up in a relationship with God. For the moralist this may or may not be so.

There is little about morality in these pages. The primary concern of the saints is with fruit. The morality of which Law speaks has nothing in common with fruit, unless it be its plastic counterpart which we sometimes see – deceiving, perhaps, for a while, but later standing self-revealed. The morality which is pleasing to God is joyful and warm and vibrant, flowing directly out of the depth of our relationship with him. 'It is as if God were to produce a fresh, green tree out of a dry log,' writes Martin Luther, 'which tree would then bear its natural fruit' (30).

Following the thought from Boehme to which Law directs us, the Christian life may be considered as a movement from the attitude of the elder brother in Jesus' best-loved parable to that of the younger son; or equally from the outlook of the Pharisee in the temple to that of the publican. In either case, the one whom Jesus commends is content – without excuse – to present himself before God as he is, his heart open to the inflowing of the divine mercy. Here is the primary secret of the joy of the saints of which our title speaks; a heart wide open to God and stripped of all desire for self-justification. It is deep in our human nature to seek to justify ourselves for our conduct, and it is likely that much self-examination of conscience, however worthy the pretext we may present, is a disguised attempt to reveal that our actions were more worthy than we now fear them to be. Jean-Pierre de Caussade gives the great rule which governs the lives of the saints: 'Leave the past to the infinite mercy of God, the future to his good providence; give the present wholly to his love by being faithful to his grace' (4). The moment we can throw ourselves freely and gladly on the goodness of God – and a lifetime of moments may first be necessary – with no side-glances towards merits as though to qualify us for his acceptance, at that moment pride will dissolve into humility, wrath into meekness, envy into gladness for another's joy, and every obstacle to the free movement of the grace of God in our hearts will be removed. 'As men without anything at all,' writes Luther, 'we must wait for the pure mercy of God' (25). 'You are endeavouring to find help in yourself and your works', writes Caussade to a sister under his direction, 'and to satisfy your conscience as if your works give your conscience greater security and stronger support than the mercy of God and the merits of Jesus Christ. I pray God to enlighten you.'[1] The theme, here illustrated from two different traditions of the Church, is one which recurs often in these pages. It is a striking fact that the saints, though they come from separated Churches, so often speak with one voice.

The depth of God's compassion

To the saints belongs the awareness that the depth of God's compassion and mercy is beyond our human capacity to understand. 'As a handful of sand thrown into the ocean,' writes St Isaac of Syria, 'so are the sins of all flesh as compared with the mind of God'(128). God's compassion, he goes on to tell us, can never be outdone by the greatness of man's sin. In their experience of forgiveness of sins and daily renewal in grace, the hearts of the saints inevitably reach out in compassion to all. We shall find much evidence of this in the readings which follow, but very especially from those taken from the two books in the series which draw on the writings of Mother Julian of Norwich. Compassion, she tells us, exercised in love, is a true mark of Christ's indwelling (254). It is not that we may not take note of another's sin where that is appropriate, but rather, that a judgemental attitude will always harm. 'Looking at another's sin', she writes, 'clouds the eyes of the soul, hiding for the time being the fair beauty of God – unless we look upon this sinner with contrition with him, compassion on him, and a holy longing to God for him' (254).

God does not blame

It was an important part of Julian's showings and contrary to what she had been led to believe through the teachings of the Church, that God does not blame us for our sins. 'I saw our Lord putting no more blame upon us than if we were as clean and as holy as the angels in heaven' (273). Julian, we remember, is writing for her 'even-Christians', that is to say for people like ourselves, aware of our many failings, yet longing to serve God better, or, in Julian's own words, 'for-men and women who, for God's love, hate sin and turn themselves to do God's will' (232). For such people, Julian sees clearly that self-blame, especially where it is prolonged, will create a serious stumbling-block to growth in Christ. 'Our good Lord Jesus Christ', she reminds us, 'has taken upon himself all our blame, and therefore our Father may not, does not wish to assign more blame to us than to his own beloved Son, Jesus Christ.'[2] Or again, 'God looks upon his servant with pity, and not with blame' (346).

Julian's picture is that after a fall her 'even-Christians' should make a brief act of contrition and then go upon their way without looking back in self-recrimination (305 and 321). That, surely, is the way of the saints: 'Lord, you know this is like me, and apart from your grace I may fall many times'; and then, without more ado, in loving confidence, a renewed turning to God. It is this filial trust in God who receives them blameless ever anew, which is the secret of their peace and joy. And it is for want of this trust that we their fellow-Christians may be besieged by guilts and fears which seriously stand in the way of God's drawing us into a closer fellowship with himself. It behoves us, therefore, to take Julian's teaching seriously, and not to shelter under a supposed humility, which is, in fact, none other than an inverted pride. The primary meaning of the Greek word for forgiveness (*aphesis*) is release, in this context release from guilt and fear. Julian was greatly concerned to tell her readers that it is not God who would bind us, but rather that we, through want of faith in his promises, so often stand in the way of his releasing us from our bonds.

The constancy of God's love

Another important element of Julian's thought, and we shall find it, too, in William Law, is that God's love is pure compassion, free in every circumstance from any element of wrath. As Julian quite simply puts it, and the sentiment is variously expressed no less than ten times, 'no anger is found in him' (130). Whether wrath in relation to God should have a place in our human vocabulary, lest compassion should degenerate into sentimentality, may be open to question. What is certain is that in God's vocabulary, the word, as we understand it, has no place in relation to himself. 'God is always constant in love,' writes Julian (310). She even says, when speaking with strict theological accuracy, that from God's point of view there can be no forgiveness of our sins,[3] meaning that forgiveness would imply a change of attitude on God's part, whereas it is in us that the change must take place. God's forgiveness is, in fact, always extended towards us – this is the point Julian is concerned to emphasize – even when we are in our sins; yet we can, of course, only appropriate that forgiveness when we turn to him again. This is but an echo of the teaching from the cross, the prayer of Jesus being uttered before there was any movement of sorrow or repentance on the part of those responsible for his death.

xiv

It may be that we need to sound a note of warning here. Julian's message of compassion and hope is not to mean that we may take sin lightly, as though it hardly matters. Julian is no sentimentalist. 'Sin', she says, 'is the sharpest lash that any chosen soul can be struck with.'[4] And again, 'I was shown no harder hell than sin.'[5] Julian believes firmly in hell but she knows that it is our wrath – by which is meant everything in us which is opposed to peace and love (333) – and not God's which may take us there, the wrath in ourselves which we have not allowed God's compassionate love to quench. Furthermore, the wrath-free character of God does not mean that we shall not suffer as our natures are cleansed in the purifying fire of his love. What it means is that in our suffering God is on our side. And it is this which makes the difference between hope and despair.

Forgiving one another

It must follow from what has been said that another mark of the saints will be their spontaneity in forgiveness. 'I cannot believe', writes St Teresa of Avila, 'that one who has approached so near to Mercy Himself, who has shown the soul what it really is and all that God has pardoned it, would not instantly and most willingly forgive, and be at peace, and remain well-affected towards anyone who has injured her' (64). This is not the language of the world, but it is that of Christ and his saints. 'Don't imagine that you will be forgiven', writes St Augustine (114), 'if you don't wholeheartedly forgive.' But how? Teresa has given us the answer: we forgive out of the fullness of the knowledge of our own infirmities. Once 'Mercy Himself' has revealed the depth of our need, and has done his own pardoning and cleansing work within, forgiveness will spontaneously flow rather than be simply the expression of obedience to a moral command. This last is not to be despised where the intention is good, and God will accept it and work upon it. Yet it needs, I think, to be said that it may take the one who so responds perilously close to the false morality against which William Law has warned. We are, perhaps, resolved to conform to an accepted Christian pattern, and our behavioural response may be little more than a means – unconscious, it may well be – of preserving an acceptable image for our own inspection and that of others in our circle. It is a response which may easily open us to the dangers of self-deception, carrying within it the seeds of patronage and condescension. True forgiveness proceeds from the heart, and where the heart is not ready, the desire to forgive – if only as a mustard seed – must be nurtured in prayer. The rest will follow as, in the words of St John of the Cross, 'God takes the soul into his own hands' to 'purify it in the dark fire' (23). The saints will always forgive others as those who know that they themselves stand in the need of the forgiveness of their fellow men and women.

God alone the source of love

The forgiveness of the saints is but a reflection of God's own forgiving love. All love begins with God; our love is but a response. We love him because he first loved us.[6] The pages of this book ring out with the message of the prevenient love of God. 'God alone is that spring of love whose supply never fails,' writes St Isaac of Syria (8). 'God is love,' writes

William Law (26), 'yea, all love; and so all love that nothing but love can come from him.' It is this all-embracing love of God, shed abroad in their hearts – strong and true, compassionate and enduring – which is the mark of the love of the saints. There is no limit to its range. It sees 'all men alike' as 'kinsmen and none as strangers . . . as friends and none as enemies' (265). Nor is it content to wait for the softening of another's heart, but sets to work at once to bring this end about. 'Pour in love', writes St John of the Cross in a memorable phrase, 'where there is no love, and you will draw love out' (308). And in the end it is all that matters. 'In the evening', says St John again, 'they will examine you in love' (*Sayings of Light and Love*, Maxim 57).

Learning to live with one another

The author of *The Cloud of Unknowing* provides a thought which occurs not infrequently in the writings of the saints. 'The perfect worker', he writes, 'regards all who hurt and maltreat him in this life as his best and special friends' (265). Is there a note of exaggeration here? I think not, and that if the author were challenged he would want to defend his claim. William Law's reading on page 318 may help us to understand. Law says (quoting and then developing his thought) that if our anger or bitterness is aroused against another, it is a natural inclination to blame this other as though he or she were responsible for injecting this passion within us. Far from it, says Law. The wrath and resentment were already there, lurking below consciousness, unrecognized it may well have been. Our companion has simply acted as a catalyst, bringing by his behaviour these our passions to the surface and thus enabling them to be seen for what they are. Rightly dealt with, the poison may now be drawn, and the way is open for a measure of healing and integration to take place. Hence it is not strange that the 'perfect worker' should be grateful for his difficult companion who has unintentionally become the means of helping him on his way. It is worth reflecting that there will be occasions when we shall all be 'difficult companions' to one another.

Archbishop William Temple has said that if we pray for patience we must expect God to answer our prayer by giving us opportunities in which to exercise it. All of us provide others, and they us, with opportunities for patience and it is thus partly through our very weaknesses that, in spite of ourselves, we may be used to help one another towards the perfection of love. St Francis de Sales and St John of the Cross both have illustrations to the effect that members of religious communities polish one another like rough stones rubbing together in the pocket. The illustration has a natural extension to home life, and beyond to every situation where people have to rub shoulders together. The phrase itself can hardly be accidental. Law concludes, 'As we are in ourselves, such is our outward sound, whatever strikes us. If our inward state is the renewed life of Christ within us, then every thing and occasion, let it be what it will, only makes the same life to sound forth and show itself.'

The understanding of divine justice

The saints are full of surprises. Perhaps no passage will come more strangely to the reader than that on page 36 from St Isaac of Syria. 'Do not speak of God as "just",' he writes, 'for his justice is not in evidence in his actions towards you . . . How can someone call God "just" when he comes across the story of the prodigal son who frittered away all his belongings in riotous living – yet merely in response to his contrition his father ran and fell on his neck, and gave him authority over all his possessions?' Certainly from the angle of the world we must call the father's action unjust, and the fractious elder brother was quick to point that out. But we are here in the realm of paradox. Just as Paul speaks of the foolishness of God as being wiser than the wisdom of men, so we might say that the injustice of God is more just than the justice of men. Paul was working out this paradox in his atonement theology, God reckoning the guilty as righteous by virtue of their faith in Christ. So different is God's justice from that of the world that we, looking at it from our human standpoint, have to find another word for it and we call it mercy. For us, mercy and justice exist in tension. In God they are integrated and become one.

In view of what has been written earlier on the wrath-free nature of God, it may be of interest to pursue our line of thought and propound a further paradox and say that just as the 'foolishness' of God is wiser than the wisdom of men, and the 'injustice' of God is more just than the justice of men, so the 'wrath' of God is more compassionate than the compassion of men. We may see the divine 'wrath' as the ceaseless energy of God's holy love which refuses to let us go, in whatever state we may be. Or, as another writer has described it, as God's relentless compassion pursuing us when we are at our worst.[7]

Still with unhurrying chase,
And unperturbèd pace,
Deliberate speed, majestic instancy,
Came on the following Feet,
And a Voice above their beat –
'Naught shelters thee, who will not shelter Me.'[8]

Doing all for God's sake

Although many of the writers portrayed here are called to prominent tasks in the way of administration, or teaching, or pastoral work, sanctity for the most part does not consist in doing unusual things but in doing usual things in an unusual way. Brother Lawrence, working for many years in the obscurity of a monastery kitchen, provides perhaps the best illustration from these pages. 'Our sanctification', he tells us, 'does not depend on our changing our work, but in doing that for God's sake which commonly we do for our own' (319). It is not the greatness of the work which matters to God but the love with which it is done (163). Three times he seems to be telling us that all perfection is contained simply in being able to pick up a straw solely for the love of God. Luther takes up the same theme. 'God pays no heed to the insignificance of the work being done, but looks at the heart which is serving him in the work; and this is true of such mundane tasks as washing the dishes or milking the cows' (38. See also 122). Thus, for the saints, in offering every action to God, life becomes, in Origen's famous phrase, 'one great unbroken prayer'. 'All that a Christian does, even in eating and sleeping,' writes John Wesley, 'is prayer when it is done in simplicity according to the order of God' (190).

xx

Referring all to God

In making the same point as the earlier writers, St John of the Cross adds an important principle. 'The heart . . . must not rest in the joy, comfort, delight and advantages which holy habits and good works bring with them. It must refer all to God' (111). For most of us it is easier to take our sorrows to God than our joys. It is a purpose of trials to enable us to discover the insufficiency of our own resources, and to seek our strength from God. Churches are fuller in wartime than in times of peace. God is our hope and strength, a very present help in troubles. Perhaps that is why we need so many. God might give us more joys if we knew how to handle them. It is a mark of the saints that they find their rest in the God of joys rather than in the joys of God. Joys have a way of evaporating when we clasp them to ourselves. Even more than that, we are left flat, in a sort of spiritual lethargy, turned in upon ourselves. It is praise and thanksgiving which are the safeguards here. William Blake captures this insight when he writes:

> He who bends to himself a joy,
> Doth the wingèd life destroy.
> But he who kisses a joy as it flies
> Lives in eternity's sunrise.

The joy of the saints

The spirit of joy breathes through the pages which follow. Joy and happiness are often used interchangeably, and the dictionaries do not appear to quarrel with this. The words, however, have separate Greek origins, and I fancy that for most people they vibrate differently. Joy has overtones of exultation of spirit, of triumph and victory. Happiness speaks more to situations of success, satisfaction or prosperity. Happiness varies with the weather, the bank balance, the opinion of others and much more. Joy, as the saints experience it, transcends these variations in our fortunes. Tasks can be undertaken and temptations conquered in the power of joy which would otherwise be too much for us. Jesus bequeathed his joy to the disciples – 'that my joy might remain in you, and that your joy might be full'[9] – and did so at a time when a full measure of suffering and hardship lay ahead. As Nehemiah has it: 'The joy of the Lord is your strength.'[10]

Joy is God's gift, second only to love in the fruit of the Spirit listed by Paul. How can it be ours? I find it interesting to note that although the word joy (or its derivatives) appears about fifty times in St Paul's epistles, nowhere does Paul tell his readers to be joyful. Instead he tells them to rejoice, and that is a different matter. Joyfulness belongs to the emotions, rejoicing to the will. You cannot feel joyful to order any more than you can fly. What you can do is to rejoice. You can praise God and go on praising him, you can recite psalms or sing hymns, you can say an office of the Church or attend a Eucharist, you can dance and sing, and in the long run your emotions will follow your will. If you are a musician you can sound the praises of God on the instrument of your skill. Those who use the rosary may find that ordinarily a fit of the blues will be dispelled in about half an hour, though that will be the consequence and not the object of the exercise. But it is best not to wait for such moods to arise. Jesus tells us that we are to watch and pray that we may not enter into temptation, rather than that it may be dispersed when it is upon us. Paul writes to the Ephesians: '. . . speaking to yourselves in psalms and hymns and spiritual songs, singing and making melody in your hearts to the Lord . . .'[11] In almost identical language he writes to the church at Colossae.[12] To the Church at Philippi, he writes: 'Rejoice in the Lord alway, and again I say, rejoice.'[13] The Psalms are full of such advice. 'Sing unto the Lord a new song.'[14] 'Praise the Lord, O my soul.'[15] 'Praise him in the sound of the trumpets.'[16] None of this is to suggest that there shall be an artificial whipping-up of the emotions, which is always to be avoided. It is rather that psalmody or its substitute serves to set the heart and mind and will anew upon God who is the one sufficient source of peace and joy.

Prayer

It was said earlier that the primary concern of the saints was with fruit, and the observation may be allowed to stand in its context. But it was the desire for union with God, the ground of their being and the end of their becoming, which was the overwhelming passion of their lives. 'You have made us for yourself,' cries Augustine (1), 'and our heart is restless till it rests in you.' As for fruit, it will take care of itself as the unitive bond is brought to perfection. God may be discovered within every Christian activity but it is in prayer above all that he will be found. It is in prayer that we are taught to be. Being matters more than doing, not because doing is unimportant but because right doing springs from right being. In prayer there is a steady exposure of the soul

xxiii

to God wherein its impurities are purged in the fire of the divine love. 'Prayer', observes St Francis de Sales (271), 'brings the mind into the brightness of the divine light and the will to the warmth of divine love.' There, he tells us, the mind is purged of ignorance and the will of wrong inclinations. It is in the place of prayer, says St John of the Cross (59), 'that God enlightens the soul, making it see not only its misery and meanness, but also his grandeur and majesty.' The experience, he emphasizes, is as of night, but from the darkness springs self-knowledge, and with that as foundation there comes the knowledge of God. There can be no Christian life without the undergirding of prayer, yet prayer is God's gift and the most we can do is to dispose ourselves to receive it. We are as the servants at Cana, bidden to fill the pots with water, and we are to fill them to the brim. We can then but wait on the breathing of the Spirit, for the wine-making belongs to him. 'Contemplation', writes St John of the Cross (59), and it is this of which we have been speaking, 'is nothing else but a secret, peaceful and loving infusion of God, which, if admitted, will set the soul on fire with the spirit of love.'

Loving confidence in God

Finally, and it links with what has just been said, the saints are those in whom abandonment to God is near to being made complete. 'Jesus points out to me the only way which leads to Love's furnace,' writes St Thérèse of Lisieux. 'That way is self-surrender – it is the confidence of the little child who sleeps without fear in its father's arms' (217). The theme is a favourite of Caussade's and a number of references will be found in this book. It is indeed the way to which Jesus points: 'He who loses his life for my sake shall find it.'[17] I recall when I was newly ordained being pulled up sharply when I misquoted this verse, saying that Jesus said that we must lose our lives in order to find them. In fact he said no such thing. We are not bidden to die in order that we may live – this is to be no nicely calculated venture embarked upon in order to bring in rich returns – but rather, in the Pauline phrase, it is a matter of 'dying and *behold* we live'.[18] What is asked of us looks like loss, has every appearance of loss, and in the nakedness of faith the plunge is taken. Jesus did not die upon the cross in order that he might rise again. He died, was truly dead, and *behold* God raised him. Here is an illustration which has application to every aspect of the Christian life. With St Paul the saints die daily, and with every death there is a rising to a deeper and fuller measure of the resurrection life. So by many deaths are they prepared – as we shall be too – for the final plunge into the ocean of God's love.

ROBERT LLEWELYN

1. *The Flame of Divine Love*, 'Enfolded in Love' series, p.27.
2. *The Revelations of Divine Love*, Julian of Norwich, ch. 51.
3. *In Love Enclosed*, 'Enfolded in Love' series, p. 56.
4. Ibid., p. 41.
5. Ibid., p. 46.
6. 1 Jn 4:19.
7. *The Fire of Your Life*, Maggie Ross, p. 19. Paulist Press, USA.
8. *The Hound of Heaven*, Francis Thompson. Taken from *The Penguin Book of Religious Verse* (1963), edited by R. S. Thomas.
9. Jn 15:11.
10. Ne 8:10.
11. Ep 5:19.
12. Col 3:16.

13. Ph 4:4.
14. Ps 33:3.
15. Ps 103:1.
16. Ps 150:3.
17. Mt 10:39.
18. 2 Co 6:9.

The heart at rest

Ask the beauty of the earth, the beauty of the sky. Question the order of the stars, the sun whose brightness lights the day, the moon whose splendour softens the gloom of night. Ask of the living creatures that move in the waves, that roam the earth, that fly in the heavens.

Question all these and they will answer, 'Yes, we are beautiful'. Their very loveliness is their confession of God: for who made these lovely mutable things, but he who is himself unchangeable beauty?

Too late have I loved you, O beauty ever ancient, ever new, too late have I loved you.

I sought for you abroad, but you were within me though I was far from you. Then you touched me, and I longed for your peace, and now all my hope is only in your great mercy.

Give what you command and then command what you will.

You have made us for yourself, and our heart is restless till it rests in you. Who will grant me to rest content in you? To whom shall I turn for the gift of your coming into my heart so that I may forget all the wrong I have done, and embrace you alone, my only good?

Augustine

The spirit of love

All religion is the spirit of love; all its gifts and graces are the gifts and graces of love; it has no breath, no life, but the life of love.

Nothing exalts, nothing purifies but the fire of love; nothing changes death into life, earth into heaven, men into angels, but love alone.

Love breathes the spirit of God; its words and works are the inspiration of God. Love speaks not of itself, but the Word, the eternal Word of God speaks in it. All that love speaks, that God speaks, because love is God.

Love is heaven revealed in the soul; it is light and truth; it is infallible; it has no errors, for all errors are the want of love.

Love has no more of pride than light has of darkness; it stands and bears all its fruit from a depth and root of humility.

Love is of no sect or party; it neither makes nor admits of any bounds; you may as easily enclose the light or shut up the air of the world in one place, as confine love to a sect or party. It lives in the liberty, the universality, the impartiality of heaven.

William Law

The nature of faith

Abraham closed his eyes and hid himself in the darkness of faith, and therein he found light eternal.

In utter despair of everything, save Christ.

Faith is a free surrender and a joyous wager on the unseen, untried and unknown goodness of God.

If you believe, you already have God; if you do not believe, you do not have him. To have faith is to have God.

Faith unites the soul with the invisible, ineffable, unutterable, eternal, unthinkable word of God, while at the same time it separates it from all things visible and tangible.

Faith alone is able, under trial, to hear the deep, secret 'Yea' of God beneath and above his 'Nay'.

That most sweet stirring of the heart.

It is a living fountain springing up into life everlasting, as Christ describes it in John 4.

Martin Luther

The providential ordering of life

To escape the distress caused by regret for the past or fear about the future, this is the rule to follow: leave the past to the infinite mercy of God, the future to his good providence; give the present wholly to his love by being faithful to his grace.

When God in his goodness sends you some disappointment, one of those trials that used to annoy you so much, before everything thank him for it as for a great favour all the more useful for the great work of your perfection in that it completely overturns the work of the moment.

Try, in spite of interior dislike, to show a kind face to troublesome people, or to those who come to chatter about their troubles; leave at once prayer, reading, choir Office, in fact anything, to go where Providence calls you; and do what is asked of you quietly, peacefully, without hurry and without vexation.

Should you fail in any of these points, make immediately an act of interior humility – not that sort of humility full of uneasiness and irritation against which St Francis de Sales said so much, but a humility that is gentle, peaceful and sweet.

Jean-Pierre de Caussade

Prayer is a great blessing

How great is the good which God works in a soul when he gives it a disposition to pray in earnest, though it may not be so well prepared as it ought to be.

If that soul perseveres in spite of sins, temptations and relapses, brought about in a thousand ways by Satan, our Lord will bring it at last – I am certain of it – to the harbour of salvation, as he has brought me myself.

May His Majesty grant I may never go back and be lost!

He who gives himself to prayer is in possession of a great blessing, of which many saintly men have written – I am speaking of mental prayer – glory be to God for it!

Let him never cease from prayer who has once begun it, be his life ever so wicked; for prayer is the way to amend it, and without prayer such amendment will be much more difficult.

As to him who has not begun to pray, I implore him by the love of our Lord not to deprive himself of so great a good.

Teresa of Avila

The way of salvation for all men

There is but one salvation for all mankind, and that is the life of God in the soul. God has but one design or intent towards all mankind, and that is to introduce or generate his own life, light and spirit in them, that all may be as so many images, temples and habitations of the holy Trinity.

This is God's will to all Christians, Jews and heathens. They are all equally the desire of his heart.

Now there is but one possible way for man to attain this salvation. There is not one way for a Jew, another for a Christian and a third for a heathen. No; God is one, human nature is one, salvation is one, and the way to it is one; and that is the desire of the soul turned to God.

Suppose this desire to be awakened and fixed upon God, though in souls that never heard either of the law or gospel, and then the new birth of Christ is formed in those who never heard his name. And these are they 'that shall come from the East and the West and sit down with Abraham and Isaac in the Kingdom of God'.

William Law

The discovery of ourselves

So far as we, by true resignation to God, die to the element of selfishness and our own will, so far as by universal love we die to envy, so far as by humility we die to pride, so far as by meekness we die to wrath, so far we get away from the devil, enter into another kingdom and leave him to dwell without us in his own elements.

The greatest good that any man can do to himself is to give lease to this inward deformity to show itself, and not to strive by any art or management, either of negligence or amusement, to conceal it from him.

First, because the root of a dark fire-life within us, which is of the nature of hell, with all its elements of selfishness, envy, pride and wrath, must be in some sort discovered to us, and felt by us, before we can enough feel and enough groan under the weight of our disorder.

Repentance is but a kind of table-talk until we see so much of the deformity of our inward nature as to be in some degree frightened and terrified at the sight of it.

There must be some kind of earthquake within us, something that must rend and shake us to the bottom, before we can be enough sensible either of the state of death we are in, or enough desirous of that Saviour who alone can raise us from it.

William Law

Love from God

Love which stems from created things is like a small lamp whose light is sustained by being fed with olive-oil.

Again, it is like a river fed by rainfall; once the supply that feeds it fails, the surge of its flow abates.

But love whose cause is God is like a spring welling up from the depths: its flow never abates, for God alone is that spring of love whose supply never fails.

Isaac of Syria

Julian receives the last rites

And when I was thirty-and-a-half years old, God sent me an illness which held me three days and three nights. On the fourth night I received all the rites of Holy Church and did not think to live until day. And after this I lingered on two days and two nights. And on the third night I often thought I was dying, and so did those who were with me.

And, young as I was, I thought it was sad to die: not because of anything on earth I wanted to live for, and not because of any pain I was afraid of – for I trusted God's mercy – but because if I had lived I should have been able to love God better and for longer, so that I should know God better and love him more in the joy of heaven.

For I thought that the time I had lived here on earth was too small and too short to deserve that endless joy – it seemed like nothing.

And so I thought: 'Good Lord, if I live no longer, may it be to your glory!'

And I understood in my mind and my body that I should die. And I assented to it with my heart and will, that God's will should be my will.

Julian of Norwich

Embracing God's love

I said to those who were near me: 'Today is Judgement Day for me.' I said this because I thought I was going to die, and on the day a man dies he is judged as he shall be judged for ever, as I see it. I said this because I wanted them to love God better, and to help them to amend their short lives by this example.

All this time I thought I was going to die and it was a wonder to me, and a sort of sorrow, for I thought this showing was meant for those who were going to live.

And what I say from myself I say as from all my fellow-Christians, for I am taught by God, through this holy showing, that this is his meaning.

Therefore I pray you all, for God's sake, and tell you for your own good, that you do not let your eye dwell on the humble woman this was shown to, but let your sight go beyond and wisely, humbly and mightily behold God who, by his courteous love and endless goodness, wishes it to be widely known to comfort us all.

For it is God's will that you should embrace his love with great joy and gladness, as Jesus has shown it to you, one and all.

Julian of Norwich

Choosing love

Jesus spoke within my heart
and said:

'No one can choose whom I
love, nor how much I love
them. Love defeats sin.'

'There is no better way to
please God than to think
continually of his love.'

'How can I love you, Lord?' I asked. He answered,
'Be aware of your sins and of my love. Do not be
afraid, what a person has been in the past is not
important, what matters is what they will be in the
future. Remember Mary Magdalene, St Paul and
many other saints, before they knew me. The
dishonest I make honest, the bad I make good.'

'When I love you, I love you for ever.'

Margery Kempe

Answers to prayer

If God is slow to grant your request and you do not receive what you ask for promptly, do not be grieved, for you are not wiser than God.

When this happens to you, it is either because your way of life does not accord with your request, or because the pathways of your heart are at odds with the intention of your prayer.

Or it may be because your inner state is too childish by comparison with the magnitude of the thing you have asked for.

It is not appropriate that great things should fall easily into our hands, otherwise God's gift will be held in dishonour, because of the ease with which we obtain it.

For anything that is readily obtained is also easily lost, whereas everything which is found with toil is preserved with care.

Isaac of Syria

Knowing God

What a miserable drudgery is the service of God, unless I love the God whom I serve! But I cannot love one whom I know not. How then can I love God till I know him? And how is it possible I should know God, unless he make himself known unto me?

The whole creation speaks that there is a God. But who will show me what that God is? The more I reflect, the more convinced I am, that it is not possible for any or all the creatures to take off the veil which is on my heart, that I might discern this unknown God; to draw the curtain back which now hangs between, that I may see him who is invisible.

This veil of flesh now hides him from my sight; and who is able to make it transparent so that I may perceive, through this glass, God always before me, till I see him 'face to face'?

O my friend, how will you get one step farther, unless God reveal himself to your soul? And why should this seem a thing incredible to you that God, a Spirit, and the Father of the spirits of all flesh, should discover himself to your spirit?

John Wesley

Morning prayer

I believe, O God of all gods,
That Thou art the eternal Father of life:
I believe, O God of all gods,
That Thou art the eternal Father of love.

I believe, O Lord and God of the peoples,
That Thou art the creator of the high heavens,
That Thou art the creator of the skies above,
That Thou art the creator of the oceans below.

I believe, O Lord and God of the peoples,
That Thou art He who created my soul and set its
    warp.
Who created my body from dust and from ashes,
Who gave to my body breath and to my soul its
    possession.
    Father, bless to me my body,
    Father, bless to me my soul,
    Father, bless to me my life,
    Father, bless to me my belief.

The Celtic Tradition

The Law and the gospel related

Why are we so feeble in faith that we more readily follow the feelings of sin and death maintained by the Law than turn to the laughter and joy of the gospel? . . .

The open jaws of hell terrify us more than the open gates of heaven elate us.

One thought of our sin causes us more sadness than almost all the sermons about the merits of Christ bring us joy.

In the trial of real anguish, the conscience should think of Christ, and know absolutely nothing but Christ only.

It should then exert its powers to the utmost to put the Law out of sight and mind, as far as it possibly can, and embrace nothing but Christ and his promises.

To say this is easy, I know. But to be able to do it in the hour of temptation, when the conscience is being handled by God, is the most difficult of all tasks.

Martin Luther

The night of the soul

You may think that I am exaggerating the night of my soul. If one judged by the poems I have composed this year, it might seem that I have been inundated with consolation, that I am a child for whom the veil of faith is almost rent asunder . . . But it is not a veil . . . it is a wall which reaches to the very heavens, shutting out the starry sky.

When I sing in my verses of the happiness of heaven and of the eternal possession of God, I feel no joy. I sing out of what I wish to believe. Sometimes, I confess a feeble ray of sunshine penetrates my dark night and brings me a moment's relief, but after it has gone, the remembrance of it, instead of consoling me, makes the blackness seem denser still.

And yet I have never experienced more fully the sweetness and mercy of the Lord. He did not send this heavy cross when it would, I believe, have discouraged me, but chose a time when I was able to bear it. Now it does no more than deprive me of all natural satisfaction in my longing for heaven.

Thérèse of Lisieux

On friendship

Love is the chief among the passions of the soul; it draws all things to itself and makes us like the one we love. Take care to admit no evil love lest you soon become evil yourself.

Friendship is the most dangerous of all love because other affections may exist without mutual communication, but since friendship is entirely founded on this, it can scarcely exist without at the same time involving participation in the qualities of the one to whom it is exercised.

All love is not friendship. We may love without being loved, and then love but not friendship exists, for friendship is mutual love, and unless it is mutual it is not friendship. Also, both the parties who love -must be aware of their reciprocal affection, otherwise it will still only be love and not friendship. Further, there must be some communication as the groundwork for friendship.

Friendship varies according to the kinds of communications, and the benefits exchanged. If these are vain and false, friendship is vain and false. If they are true, then friendship will be true. The more excellent the qualities exchanged, the higher the friendship will be.

Francis de Sales

Prayer carried in the heart

[Brother Lawrence said]:

That he was then happily employed in the cobbler's workshop; but that he was as ready to quit that post as the former, since he was always finding pleasure in every condition by doing little things for the love of God.

With him the *set* times of prayers were not different from other times.

He retired to pray, according to the direction of his Superior, but he did not want such retirement or ask for it, because his greatest business did not divert him from God.

As he knew his obligation to love God in all things, and as he endeavoured so to do, he had no need of a director to advise him, but he needed much a confessor to absolve him.

He was very sensible of his faults, but not discouraged by them.

He confessed them to God, but did not plead against him to excuse them.

When he had done so, he peaceably resumed his usual practice of love and adoration.

Brother Lawrence

Counsel on prayer

I have only two things to say on the subject of prayer:

Make it with absolute compliance with the will of God, no matter whether it be successful, or you are troubled with dryness, distractions, or other obstacles.

If it is easy and full of consolations, return thanks to God without dwelling on the pleasure it has caused you.

If it has not succeeded, submit to God, humbling yourself, and go away contented and in peace even if it should have failed through your own fault; redoubling your confidence and resignation to his holy will.

Persevere in this way and sooner or later God will give you grace to pray properly.

But whatever trials you may have to endure, never allow yourself to be discouraged.

Jean-Pierre de Caussade

The intention in prayer

The fact of being incapable of sustained thought, or of producing acts in prayer, need not sadden the soul; for the best part of prayer and the essential part is the wish to make it well.

The intention is everything in God's sight, either for good or evil; now this desire it has to the extreme of anxiety – therefore it is only too keen, and has to be moderated.

The soul must be kept peaceful during prayer and end prayer in peace.

For directing the intention the soul abandoned to God need not make many acts; neither is it obliged to express them in words.

The best thing for it is to be content to feel and to know that it is acting for God in the simplicity of its heart.

This is making good interior acts; they are made simply by the impulsion of the heart without any outward expression, almost without thinking.

The chief principle of the spiritual life is to do everything, interior as well as exterior, peacefully, gently, sweetly, as St Francis de Sales so often recommends. God sees all our desires, even the first movements of the heart.

Jean-Pierre de Caussade

The soul is guided by faith

In a dark night
With anxious love inflamed,
O happy lot!
Forth unobserved I went,
My house being now at rest.

In darkness and in safety
By the secret ladder,
  disguised,
O happy lot!
In darkness and concealment,
My house being now at rest.

On the road to union with God the night of faith shall guide me.

Faith tells us of things we have never seen, and cannot come to know by our natural senses.

The light of faith is like the light of the sun which blinds our eyes because its light is stronger than our powers of sight. So the light of faith transcends our comprehension.

John of the Cross

God's nurturing

It must be realized that usually, after conversion, the soul is spiritually nurtured and fondled by God as a little child is by its devoted mother, who warms it close to her breast, nourishes it with sweet milk and soft food, and carries and caresses it within the circle of her arms.

But as the child grows up the mother gradually ceases her caresses, sets the child down, and makes it walk on its own feet. This is in order that it may abandon the ways of childhood and direct itself to more important and substantial occupations.

The loving mother is like the grace of God, for as soon as the soul is newly awakened he treats it in the same way, giving it the breast of his tender love as if it were an infant.

But souls must realize their weakness in this state. They must take courage and desire to be brought into the night where the soul is strengthened and prepared for true love of God.

John of the Cross

The work the soul must do

Those beginners who make progress do not rely on visible instruments. They do not burden themselves with them, nor do they seek to know more than is necessary for acting rightly. Their eyes are fixed on God, and their desire is to please him.

With great generosity they give up all they possess, spiritual and material, for their joy is to be poor out of love for God and their neighbour. They set their sights only upon true interior perfection which is to please God in everything, and themselves in nothing.

It is right that the soul, as far as it is able, should work to purify itself, that it may merit that God take it into his divine care and heal it of those imperfections before which it is helpless.

For, after all the efforts of the soul, it cannot by its unaided labours make itself fitted for union with God in love. God must take it himself into his own hands and purify it in the dark fire.

John of the Cross

True humility

True humility does not affect to be humble and makes few lowly speeches, for she does not only desire to hide other virtues, but above all hide herself. So my advice is that you do not abound in expressions of humility. Never cast down your eyes without humbling your heart. Do not pretend you want to be among the last unless you truly desire it in your heart.

A really humble man would rather let another say that he is contemptible and worth nothing than say it himself. He believes it himself and is content that others should share his opinion.

Some say they fear to discredit religion if they pretend to it, because of their weaknesses. Or they will not do good to God or their neighbour for fear of pride. Such excuses are deceptive; they are false humility and evil. They seem to cloak their self-love and laziness under the guise of humility.

The proud man who trusts in himself may fear to undertake anything, but the humble are bold in proportion to the insufficiency of their own which they feel. As they acknowledge their weakness they acquire strength, because they rely on God.

Francis de Sales

Justification – on being right with God

By the one solid rock we call the doctrine of justification by faith alone, we mean that we are redeemed from sin, death and the devil, and are made partakers of life eternal, not by self-help but by outside help, namely, by the work of the only-begotten Son of God, Jesus Christ alone.

God does not want to save us by our own personal and private righteousness and wisdom. He wants to save us by a righteousness and wisdom apart from this, other than this: a righteousness which does not come from ourselves, is not brought to birth by ourselves. It is a righteousness which comes into us from somewhere else.

It is not a righteousness which finds its origins in this world of ours.

As men without anything at all, we must wait for the pure mercy of God, we must wait for him to reckon us as righteous and wise.

As long as I recognize that I can in no way be righteous in the sight of God . . . , I then begin to ask for righteousness from him.

The only thing that resists this idea of justification is the pride of the human heart, proud through unbelief.

Martin Luther

God's universal love

Some people have an idea of the Christian religion as if God was thereby declared so full of wrath against fallen man that nothing but the blood of his only begotten Son could satisfy his vengeance. These are miserable mistakers of the divine nature and miserable reproachers of his great love and goodness.

For God is love, yea, all love; and so all love that nothing but love can come from him; and the Christian religion is nothing else but an open, full manifestation of his universal love towards all mankind.

As the light of the sun has only one common nature towards all objects that can receive it, so God has only one common nature of goodness towards all created nature, breaking forth in infinite flames of love upon every part of creation and calling everything to the highest happiness it is capable of.

God so loved man, when his fall was foreseen, that he chose him to salvation in Christ Jesus before the foundation of the world. When man was actually fallen, God was so without all wrath towards him that he sent his only begotten Son into the world to redeem him. Therefore God has no nature towards man but love, and all that he does to man is love.

William Law

The wrath is in us and not in God

There is no wrath that stands between God and us but what is awakened in the dark fire of our own fallen nature; and to quench this wrath, and not his own, God gave his only begotten Son to be made man.

God has no more wrath in himself now than he had before the creation, when he had only himself to love. The precious blood of his Son was not poured out to pacify himself (who in himself had no nature towards man but love), but it was poured out to quench the wrath and fire of the fallen soul, and to kindle in it a birth of light and love.

As man lives and moves and has his being in the divine nature, and is supported by it, whether his nature be good or bad, so the wrath of man, which was awakened in the dark fire of his fallen nature, may, in a certain sense, be called the wrath of God, as hell itself may be said to be in God because nothing can be out of his immensity. Yet this hell is not God, but the dark habitation of the devil. And this wrath which may be called the wrath of God is not God, but the fiery wrath of the fallen soul.

William Law

Come, you blessed of my Father, receive a kingdom

What are we to receive? A kingdom. For doing what? 'I was hungry and you fed me.' What is more ordinary, more of this world, than to feed the hungry, and yet it rates the Kingdom of Heaven!

'Feed the hungry, take the homeless into your house, clothe the naked.' But what if you can't afford bread for the hungry, or have no house nor spare clothes? Give a cup of cold water, put two pence in the alms box. The poor widow gave as much with her two pennies as Zacchaeus did with half his fortune.

What you have is the measure of your gift. Yet many give alms to a beggar to show off, and not because they love their brother.

You stand before God: ask your own heart, look at what you did and why you did it: was it for the empty praise of men? Look at your heart, because you cannot judge what you do not see.

So, beloved, let us search our hearts in God's presence: you can hide from man, but not from God.

Flee to God himself if you want to run away from him; flee by confessing, not by hiding; say to him, 'You are my refuge', and so let the love which alone brings life grow within you.

Augustine

Grace – what it is

I am seeking, searching, thirsting for nothing else than a gracious God.

Yet God continuously and earnestly offers himself as a God of grace, and urges even those who spurn him and are his enemies, to accept him as such.

These promises of grace★ are all based on Christ from the beginning of the world, so that God promises his grace to no one in any other way than in Christ and through Christ.

Christ is the messenger of God's promise to the entire world.

Grace consists in this:
that God is merciful to us,
shows himself gracious for the sake of the
Lord Christ, forgives all sins, and will not
impute them to us for eternal death.
That is grace: the forgiveness of sins for the
sake of the Lord Christ,
the covering-up of all sins.

Grace makes the Law dear to us.
And then, sin is no more there,
and the Law is no longer against us,
but with us.

Martin Luther

★ Jn 1:17.

Grace – how it works

All the many countless blessings which God gives us here on earth are merely those gifts which last for a time.

But his grace and loving regard are the inheritance which endures throughout eternity . . .

In giving us such gifts here on earth he is giving us only those things that are his own, but in his grace and love towards us he gives his very self.

In receiving his gifts we touch but his hand; but in his gracious regard we receive his heart, his spirit, his mind, his will.

Man receives grace immediately and fully. In this way he is saved. Good works are not necessary to assist him in this: they follow. It is as if God were to produce a fresh, green tree out of a dry log, which tree would then bear its natural fruit.

Martin Luther

Our weakness and God's help

Blessed is the man who knows his own weakness, because awareness of this becomes for him the foundation and beginning of all that is good and beautiful.

For whenever someone realizes and perceives that he is truly and indeed weak, then he draws in his soul from the diffuseness which dissipates knowledge, and he becomes all the more watchful of his soul.

But no one can perceive his own weakness unless he has been remiss a little, has neglected some small thing, has been surrounded by trials, either in the matter of things which cause the body suffering, or in that of ways in which the soul is subject to the passions. Only then, by comparing his own weakness, will he realize how great is the assistance which comes from God.

When someone is aware that he is in need of divine help, he makes many prayers. And once he has made much supplication, his heart is humbled, for there is no one who is in need and asks who is not humbled. 'A broken and humbled heart, God will not despise.'*

As long as the heart is not humbled it cannot cease from wandering; for humility concentrates the heart.

Isaac of Syria

* Ps 51:17.

The nature of salvation

This great gift of God, the salvation of our souls, which is begun on earth, but perfected in heaven, is no other than the image of God fresh stamped upon our hearts. It is a renewal in the spirit of our minds after the likeness of him that created us. It is a salvation from sin, and doubt and fear.

From fear; for, 'being justified freely', they who believe 'have peace with God through Jesus Christ our Lord, and rejoice in hope of the glory of God'. From doubt; for 'the Spirit of God beareth witness with their spirit, that they are the children of God'. And from sin; for 'being now made free from sin, they are servants of righteousness'.

God hath now 'laid the axe to the root of the tree, purifying their hearts by faith, and cleansing all the thoughts of their hearts by the inspiration of his Holy Spirit'. Having this hope, that they shall soon see God as he is, they 'purify themselves as he is pure', and are 'holy as he which hath called them is holy in all manner of conversation'.

Not that they have 'already attained' all they shall attain, neither are 'already', in this sense, 'perfect'. But they daily go on 'from strength to strength'. 'Beholding now as in a glass the glory of the Lord, they are changed into the same image, from glory to glory, as by the Spirit of the Lord.'

John Wesley

Purification

On the day of purification,
which is Candlemas, all the
people were in church with
their candles and in
contemplation I saw our Lady
with Joseph offering her son
to Simeon, the priest in the
temple. I heard songs so
beautiful that I was
transported with love for our
Lord and could not hold my candle to offer to the
priest.

Every time I see women being purified after child-
birth it is as though I see our Lady.

When I watch a wedding, in my heart I see our Lady
joined with St Joseph and the joining of a soul with
Jesus Christ our Lord.

When I see children carried in their mothers' arms it
seems to me I see Christ in his childhood.

Margery Kempe

The nature of true devotion

You aim at true devotion because, as a Christian, you know how acceptable this is to God. Small errors at the beginning can become almost irreparable. First, then, you must find out the nature of this virtue, because each one can colour devotion according to taste.

One fasts, but is full of bitterness. Another will not let his tongue touch wine or even water for sobriety's sake, but does not scruple to dirty it with his neighbour's blood by calumny and detraction. Another repeats many prayers daily, but gives way to angry, proud and hurtful language among his household and neighbours. Another readily gives to the poor, but cannot forgive his enemies. These may pass as devout, but they are not.

True, living devotion presupposes the love of God; indeed, it is itself a true love of him in the highest form. Divine love, enlightening our soul and making us pleasing to God, is called grace. Giving us power to do good, it is called charity. When it reaches the point of perfection where it makes us earnestly, frequently and readily do good, it is called devotion.

Francis de Sales

Charity and devotion

Devotion is spiritual agility and vivacity, by means of which charity works in us lovingly and readily. Charity leads us to obey and fulfil all God's commandments; devotion leads us to obey them promptly and diligently. Therefore, no one who fails to observe all these commandments can be truly virtuous or devout, since to be good one must have charity, and to be devout a ready eagerness to fulfil the laws of charity.

As devotion consists in excelling charity, it not only makes us active, ready and diligent in keeping God's commandments, but it also stimulates us to the eager and loving performance of all the good works we can do, even though they are not commanded but only counselled.

Charity and devotion differ no more than the flame from the fire. Charity is a spiritual fire which breaks out into flame and is then called devotion. Devotion simply adds a flame to the fire of charity which makes it ready, active and diligent not only in keeping God's commandments, but also in carrying out the heavenly counsels and inspirations.

Francis de Sales

God's goodness

Do not hate the sinner. Become a proclaimer of God's grace, seeing that God provides for you even though you are unworthy.

Although your debt to him is very great, there is no evidence of him exacting any payment from you, whereas in return for the small ways in which you do manifest good intention, he rewards you abundantly. Do not speak of God as 'just', for his justice is not in evidence in his actions towards you.

How can you call God just when you read the gospel lesson concerning the hiring of the workmen in the vineyard? How can someone call God just when he comes across the story of the prodigal son who frittered away all his belongings in riotous living – yet merely in response to his contrition his father ran and fell on his neck, and gave him authority over all his possessions?

In these passages it is not someone else speaking about God; had that been the case, we might have had doubts about God's goodness. No, it is God's own Son who testifies about him in this way.

Where then is this 'justice' in God, seeing that, although we were sinners, Christ died for us? If he is so compassionate in this, we have faith that he will not change.

Isaac of Syria

Works of mercy

Two works of mercy set a man free: forgive and you will be forgiven, and give and you will receive.

When we pray we are all beggars before God: we stand before the great householder bowed down and weeping, hoping to be given something; and that something is God himself.

What does a poor man beg from you? Bread. What do you beg from God? – Christ, who said, 'I am the living bread which came down from heaven.'

Do you really want to be forgiven? Then forgive. Do you hope to receive something? Then give to another. And if you want your prayer to fly up to God, give it two wings, fasting and almsgiving.

But look carefully at what you do: don't think it is enough to fast if it is only penance for sin, and does not benefit someone else. You deprive yourself of something, but to whom do you give what you do without?

Fast in such a way that you rejoice to see that dinner eaten by another; not grumbling and looking gloomy, giving because the beggar wearies you rather than because you are feeding the hungry.

If you are sad when you give alms, you lose both bread and merit, because 'God loves a cheerful giver'.

Augustine

Good works

Paul sets forth the whole life of a Christian man in Galatians 5:6, namely, that inwardly it consists of faith towards God, and outwardly in charity and good works to our neighbour.

In faith all works are equal, and any one work the same as any other.

God does not consider how little, or how great the works are, but God looks on the heart, which performs in faith and obedience to God the demands of its calling.

I cannot turn my neighbour away without turning God away: and that is to fall into unbelief.

We are, if I may be allowed so to express it, Christs to our neighbour.

God pays no heed to the insignificance of the work being done, but looks at the heart which is serving him in the work; and this is true of such mundane tasks as washing the dishes or milking the cows.

Martin Luther

At the point of death

'You do not need to be afraid
of dying in pain for I will be
with you and your mind will
be fixed on me.'

'I promise that you will have
no more distress for I have
tested you for many years
with doubts and fears in
your thoughts and dreams.'

'I will take your soul into my own hands which were
nailed to the cross and offer it to my Father with
incense and music, and you will see him.'

'I shall take you by the hand and we will dance for
joy in heaven with all the saints and angels who will
rejoice at your coming.'

Margery Kempe

The ground of our praying

Prayer is the deliberate and persevering action of the soul. It is true and enduring, and full of grace. Prayer fastens the soul to God and makes it one with his will, through the deep inward working of the Holy Spirit.

I am the ground of your praying. First, it is my will that you should have this; then I make it your will, too; then I make you ask for it, and you do so. How then should you not have what you pray for?

Everything our good Lord makes us to pray for, he has ordained that we should have since before time began.

When we come to heaven, our prayers shall be waiting for us as part of our delight, with endless joyful thanks from God.

Julian of Norwich

Perseverance in prayer

Our prayer brings great joy and gladness to our Lord. He wants it and awaits it.

By his grace he can make us as like him in inward being as we are in outward form. This is his blessed will.

So he says this, 'Pray inwardly, even though you find no joy in it. For it does good, though you feel nothing, see nothing, yes, even though you think you cannot pray. For when you are dry and empty, sick and weak, your prayers please me, though there be little enough to please you. All believing prayer is precious to me.'

God accepts the goodwill and work of his servants, no matter how we feel.

It pleases God that by the help of his grace we should work away at our praying and our living, directing all our powers to him until in the fullness of joy we have him whom we seek – Jesus.

Julian of Norwich

Not to judge

A brother in Scetis committed a fault. A council was called to which abba Moses was invited, but he refused to go to it. Then the priest sent someone to him, saying, 'Come, for everyone is waiting for you.' So he got up and went. He took a leaking jug and filled it with water and carried it with him. The others came out to meet him and said, 'What is this, father?' The old man said to them, 'My sins run out behind me, and I do not see them, and today I am coming to judge the errors of another.' When they heard that, they said no more to the brother but forgave him.

A brother sinned and the priest ordered him to go out of the church; abba Bessarion got up and went out with him, saying, 'I, too, am a sinner.'

The Desert Fathers

Grace to meet every need

[Brother Lawrence said]:

That we ought to act with God in the greatest simplicity, speaking to him frankly and plainly, and imploring his assistance in our affairs just as they happen. God never failed to grant it, as he had often experienced.

He had been lately sent into Burgundy to buy the provision of wine for the Society, which was a very unwelcome task to him, because he had no turn for business, and because he was lame and could not go about the boat except by rolling himself over the casks. However, he gave himself no uneasiness about it, nor about the purchase of the wine. He said to God that it was his business he was about, and that afterwards he found it very well performed.

He had been sent into Auvergne the year before upon the same account; that he could not tell how the matter passed, but that it proved very well.

So, likewise, in his business in the kitchen (to which he had naturally a great aversion) having accustomed himself to do everything there for the love of God, and with prayer, upon all occasions, for his grace to do his work well, he had found everything easy during the fifteen years he had been employed there.

Brother Lawrence

The nature of pure love

It is true that love, even the purest, does not exclude in the soul the desire of its own salvation and perfection.

But it is equally incontestable that the nearer the soul approaches the perfect purity of divine love, the more its thoughts and reflections are turned away from itself and fixed on the infinite goodness of God.

This divine goodness does not compel us to repudiate the happiness it destines for us, but it has every right, doubtless, to be loved for itself alone without any reflection on our own interests.

This love, which includes the love of ourselves but is independent of it, is what theologians call pure love; and all agree in recognizing that the soul is so much the more perfect according to the measure in which it habitually acts under the influence of this love, and the extent to which it divests itself of all self-seeking, at any rate unless its own interests are subordinated to the interests of God.

Therefore total renunciation without reserve or limit has no thoughts of self-interest – it thinks but of God, of his good pleasure, of his wishes, of his glory.

Jean-Pierre de Caussade

The work which pleases God most

Lift up your heart to God with a humble stirring of love; and mean God himself, and not what you get from him.

Be on your guard lest you think of anything but God himself. Let nothing occupy your mind or will but only God.

Do everything you can to forget all God's creatures and their activities, so that nothing holds your mind or desire whether it be in general or particular.

Let them be, and pay no attention to them.

This is the work of the soul which pleases God more than any other. All saints and angels rejoice over it, and speed it on with all their might.

All mankind is wonderfully helped by this work – more than you can ever be aware. Yes, even the very souls in purgatory find their pains eased by virtue of it.

And you yourself are made clean and virtuous by this work as by no other.

Author of 'The Cloud of Unknowing'

A cloud of unknowing

In the power of grace, and in the strength of eager and joyful desire, this is the lightest work of all. Otherwise it is hard, and a wonder if you achieve it.

Work away, then, until desire is kindled. When you first begin you will find only darkness and, as it were, a cloud of unknowing.

You cannot tell what it is, excepting that you feel in your will a naked reaching-out to God.

This cloud and this darkness, no matter what you do, is between you and your God. It prevents you from seeing him clearly with your mind and from experiencing the sweetness of his love in your heart.

Prepare yourself to wait in this darkness as long as you may, ever calling after him whom you love.

If ever you shall feel him or see him – as far as is possible here below – it must always be in this cloud and this darkness.

If you will but work on earnestly as I bid you, I believe that in his mercy you will win through.

Author of 'The Cloud of Unknowing'

The cloud of forgetting

Just as this cloud of unknowing is above you and between you and your God, so too you must put a cloud of forgetting beneath you and between you and all created things.

It may, perhaps, seem to you that you are a long way off from God because of this cloud of unknowing between you and him.

But surely, if the truth be told, you are much further from him when you have no cloud of forgetting between him and all his creatures.

When I speak of God's creatures I mean not them only, whether bodily or spiritual, but also their state and their works, whether good or evil.

In short, I tell you, everything is to be hidden under the cloud of forgetting.

Author of 'The Cloud of Unknowing'

The effects of devotion

The world runs down devotion, representing devout people as gloomy, sad and irritable in appearance, pretending that religion creates melancholy and unsociable people. But the Holy Spirit, speaking by all the saints and our Lord himself, assures us that the devout life is a lovely, pleasant and happy life.

The world sees only how the devout fast, pray and bear reproach; how they nurse the sick, give alms to the poor, restrain their temper and perform similar actions, which in themselves and taken alone are hard and painful. But the world does not see the heart's interior devotion which renders these actions agreeable, easy and pleasant.

Look at the bees; they suck bitter juice from thyme and by their nature convert it into honey. Devout souls find many hardships, it is true, in their works of mortification, but in doing them, they convert bitterness into sweetness.

True devotion is a spiritual sugar which takes away the bitterness of mortification, and the danger of gratification; it counteracts the poor man's discontent and the rich man's self-satisfaction; the loneliness of the oppressed and the vainglory of the successful, the sadness of the one who is alone and the dissipation of the one in society.

Francis de Sales

Devotion is varied according to calling

In creation, God commanded
the plants to bring forth
fruit each according to its
kind. Similarly, God
commands Christians to
bring forth the fruits of
devotion according to each
one's calling and vocation.
The practice of devotion
must be adapted to the capabilities, the engagements
and the duties of each individual.

It would not do for a bishop to adopt a Carthusian
solitude, or the father of a family to refuse to save
money like a Franciscan; for a workman to spend his
whole time in church like a professional religious; or
for a religious to be always exposed to interruptions
on his neighbour's behalf as a bishop must be. Such
devotion would be inconsistent and ridiculous.

True devotion hinders no one. Rather, it perfects
everything. Whenever it is out of keeping with any
person's calling, it must be false. Aristotle says that
the bee extracts honey from flowers without injuring
them, leaving them as fresh and as whole as it finds
them. True devotion does better still; it hinders no
duty or vocation, but adorns and beautifies them.

Francis de Sales

Blessing of the kindling

I will kindle my fire this morning
In the presence of the holy angels of heaven,
In the presence of Ariel of the loveliest form,
In the presence of Uriel of the myriad charms,
Without malice, without jealousy, without envy,
Without fear, without terror of anyone under
　　the sun,
But the Holy Son of God to shield me.
　　　Without malice, without jealousy, without
　　　　envy,
　　　Without fear, without terror of anyone under
　　　　the sun,
　　　But the Holy Son of God to shield me.

God, kindle Thou in my heart within
A flame of love to my neighbour,
To my foe, to my friend, to my kindred all,
To the brave, to the knave, to the thrall,
O Son of the loveliest Mary,
From the lowliest thing that liveth,
To the Name that is highest of all.

The Celtic Tradition

Trust in God

The Spirit of God spoke to me and said:

'Go in the name of Jesus. I will go with you to help and support you in all you do. Trust me, you have never found me wanting. I will never ask you to do anything that is unacceptable to God.'

'I am your God and I delight in you, we shall never be parted. All the promises I have made to you will come true at the right time.'

The Lord Jesus Christ who is always ready to help and never deserts those who truly love him said, 'Do not be afraid, I will give you all you need.'

I know the Lord will help because he has never failed me wherever I have been. I have complete trust in him.

Margery Kempe

Grace abounding

Wherewithal then shall a sinful man atone for any the least of his sins? With his own works? No. Were they ever so many or holy, they are not his own, but God's. But indeed they are all unholy and sinful themselves, so that every one of them needs a fresh atonement.

Only corrupt fruit grows on a corrupt tree. And his heart is altogether corrupt and abominable, being 'come short of the glory of God', the glorious righteousness at first impressed on his soul, after the image of his great Creator. Therefore, having nothing, neither righteousness nor works, to plead, his mouth is utterly stopped before God.

If, then, sinful men find favour with God, it is 'grace upon grace'. If God vouchsafe still to pour fresh blessings upon us, yea, the greatest of all blessings, salvation; what can we say to these things but, 'Thanks be unto God for his unspeakable gift!'

And thus it is. Herein 'God commendeth his love towards us in that, while we were yet sinners, Christ died' to save us. 'By grace', then, 'are you saved through faith.' Grace is the source, faith the condition of salvation.

John Wesley

On the practice of external mortification

I do not approve of those who begin reforming a person with external things – hair, face or dress. On the contrary, we must begin from within. 'Turn to me with your whole heart' is God's call. 'My son, give me your heart.' For the heart is the mainspring of our actions. So our Lord says: 'Set me a seal upon your heart and a seal upon your arm', for whoever truly has Jesus Christ in his heart will soon show it in all his outward actions.

If he is in your heart, he will also be in all your gestures, in your eyes, in your mouth, your hands, so that you may say with St Paul, 'It is no longer I who live, but Christ who lives in me' (Galatians 2:20). But this same heart needs to be trained in its outward demeanour. So, if you can fast, you will do well to observe some abstinence beyond the Church's law, to elevate your spirit, subdue the flesh, strengthen virtue.

Labour and fasting weary and exhaust the flesh. If your labour is necessary or serviceable to the glory of God, I should select for you the discipline of labour in preference to that of fasting. One finds his labour in fasting, another in nursing the sick, visiting prisoners, hearing confessions, comforting the afflicted, prayer. Those labours are of more avail than fasting, for while they subdue the flesh they bring forth excellent fruit.

Francis de Sales

The heart's delight

First return to yourself from what is outside you, and then give yourself back to him who made you; for he is the sum of all our happiness and our perfect good. To worship him is to love him, to long to see him, and to hope and believe that you will see him. This is to long for happiness – to reach him is happiness itself.

Ask yourself how much your love has increased: the answer your heart gives is the measure of your advancement. We now see him confusedly, as our love increases – but then we shall see him clearly.

Beloved, this love does not come to us of our own free choice, but by the Holy Spirit who has been given to us; for how could we have cleaved to God if he had not spoken to our hearts?

At the last we shall all receive the reward of salvation, like the labourers in the vineyard who came at different times, yet all were given the same wage. With the prophets, apostles and martyrs we shall contemplate the glory of God, and looking in his face sing his praises for ever. There will be no more sin, no more falsehood, and in love we shall cleave to him for whom we now sigh. We shall live for ever in that city whose light is God, finding in him that happiness we now labour for.

Augustine

It is necessary to help ourselves

How can we doubt that God understands our requirements better than we do ourselves, and that his arrangements are most advantageous to us although we do not comprehend them? But perhaps you ask that if it is sufficient for us passively to submit to being led, then what about the proverb 'God helps those who help themselves'?

I did not say that you were to do nothing – without doubt it is necessary to help ourselves; to wait with folded arms for everything to drop from heaven is according to natural inclination, but would be an absurd and culpable quietism applied to supernatural grace. Therefore while co-operating with God and leaning on him, you must never leave off working yourself.

When, in all our actions, we look upon ourselves as instruments in the hands of God to work out his hallowed designs, we shall act quietly, without anxiety, without hurry, without uneasiness about the future, without troubling about the past, giving ourselves up to the fatherly providence of God and relying more on him than on all possible human means.

In this way we shall always be at peace, and God will infallibly turn everything to our good, whether temporal or eternal.

Jean-Pierre de Caussade

Be of good cheer

Do not despair of yourselves. You are men, made in the image of God, and he who made you men was himself made man; the blood of the only begotten Son was shed for you. If, thinking of your frailty, you hold yourselves cheap, value yourselves by the price that was paid for you.

I ask you what you believe in, not what you live up to: you will answer that you believe in Christ.

Your faith is your righteousness; because if you believe, you are on your guard, if you are on your guard, you try; and God knows your endeavour and sees your goodwill, and waits for your striving, and supports your faintness, and crowns your victory.

The Lord knows who are his own, like the farmer who sees the grain among the chaff. Don't be afraid that you will not be recognized, that storms will blow the grain under the chaff. The judge is not some countryman with a pitchfork, but the triune God. He is the God of Abraham, Isaac and Jacob, but he is your God too. You ask him for your reward and the giver is himself the gift. What more can you want?

Augustine

Prayer and pride

I know a very old nun of most exemplary life in every way – would to God my life were like hers! – very holy, very austere, and a perfect religious, who has spent many hours for several years in vocal prayers, but cannot make use of mental prayer: the utmost she can do is to pause a little, from time to time (during her Ave Marias and Paternosters). Many people resemble her.

If they are humble, I do not think they are more imperfect or believe they will be any the worse for it in the end but quite as well off as those who enjoy many consolations.

In one way such souls are safer, for we cannot tell whether spiritual delights come from God or from the devil; if they are not divine they are very dangerous, for Satan tries to excite pride by their means: however, if they are sent by God there is nothing to fear for they bring humility with them.

Teresa of Avila

The night of sense*

There are three tests to ascertain whether dryness in prayer is the result of God's purgation or of our own sins.

The first is when we find no comfort either in the things of God or in created things. For when God brings the soul into the dark night in order to wean it from sweetness and to purify its sensual desires, he does not allow it to find sweetness or comfort anywhere.

The second is that the memory is ordinarily centred on God with painful anxiety and carefulness. The spirit becomes strong, more vigilant and more careful lest there be any negligence in serving God.

The third sign is inability to meditate or make reflections, and to excite the imagination as before, despite all the efforts we may make. For God now begins to communicate himself, no longer through the channels of sense as formerly, but in pure spirit.

John of the Cross

---

* John of the Cross is often referred to as the Doctor of the Dark Night. This is because, as John saw it, the path to God can only be a way of darkness. Nothing we see, feel or imagine can put us into contact with his infinity. Faith demands that we allow God to purge our senses and go by a way that is dark to human knowledge. The nights of sense and spirit are both aspects of this one refining process as God works on us at ever deeper and incomprehensible levels.

More of the same

I do not mean to lay down a general rule for the cessation of meditation; that should occur when meditation is no longer feasible, and only then, when our Lord, either in the way of purgation and affliction, or of the most perfect contemplation, shall make it impossible.

At other times, and on other occasions, this help must be had recourse to, namely, meditation on the life and passion of Christ, which is the best means of purification and of patience and security on the road, and an admirable aid to the highest contemplation.

Contemplation is nothing else but a secret, peaceful and loving infusion of God, which, if admitted, will set the soul on fire with the spirit of love.

God enlightens the soul, making it see not only its misery and meanness, but also his grandeur and majesty.

Thus out of this night springs first the knowledge of oneself, and on that, as a foundation, is built up the knowledge of God.

John of the Cross

Joyous death

Give Thou to me, O God,
The death of the priceless oil;
Give Thou to me, O God,
That the Healer of my soul be near me;
Give Thou to me, O God,
The death of joy and of peace.

Give Thou to me, O God,
To confess the death of Christ;
Give Thou to me, O God,
To meditate the agony of Christ;
Give Thou to me, O God,
To make warm the love of Christ.

O great God of Heaven,
Draw Thou my soul to Thyself
That I may make repentance
With a right and a strong heart,
With a heart broken and contrite,
That shall not change nor bend nor yield.

O great God of the angels,
Bring Thou me to the dwelling of peace;
O great God of the angels,
Preserve me from the evil of the fairies;
O great God of the angels,
Bathe me in the bathing of Thy pool.

The Celtic Tradition

Benediction

Glorious Lord, I give you greeting!
Let the church and the chancel praise you,
Let the chancel and the church praise you,
Let the plain and the hillside praise you,
Let the world's three well-springs praise you,
Two above wind and one above land,
Let the dark and the daylight praise you.
Abraham, founder of the faith, praised you:
Let the life everlasting praise you,
Let the birds and honeybees praise you,
Let the shorn stems and the shoots praise you.
Both Aaron and Moses praised you:
Let the male and the female praise you,
Let the seven days and the stars praise you,
Let the air and the ether praise you,
Let the books and the letters praise you,
Let the fish in the swift streams praise you,
Let the thought and the action praise you,
Let the sand-grains and the earth-clods praise you,
Let all the good that's performed praise you.
And I shall praise you, Lord of glory:
Glorious Lord, I give you greeting!

The Celtic Tradition

Mortification barren without love

[Brother Lawrence said]:

That all mortifications and other exercises were only useful in so far as they advanced union with God by love.

He had well considered this, and found it the shortest way to go straight to him by a continual practice of love and doing all things for his sake.

All possible kinds of mortification, if they were devoid of the love of God, could not efface a single sin.

We ought without anxiety to expect the pardon of our sins from the blood of Jesus Christ, labouring simply to love him with all our hearts.

God seemed to have granted the greatest favours to the greatest sinners, as more signal monuments of his mercy.

He thought neither of death nor of his sins, nor heaven nor hell, but of doing little things – being incapable of big ones – for the love of God. He had no need to trouble himself further, for whatever followed would be pleasing to God.

Brother Lawrence

St Kevin and the blackbird

At one Lenten season, St Kevin, as was his way, fled from the company of men to a certain solitude, and in a little hut that did but keep out the sun and the rain, gave himself earnestly to reading and to prayer, and his leisure to contemplation alone. And as he knelt in his accustomed fashion, with his hand outstretched through the window and lifted up to heaven, a blackbird settled on it, and busying herself as in her nest, laid in it an egg. And so moved was the saint that in all patience and gentleness he remained, neither closing nor withdrawing his hand: but until the young ones were fully hatched he held it out unwearied, shaping it for the purpose.

The Celtic Tradition

True prayer results in ready forgiveness

I cannot believe that one who has approached so near to Mercy Himself, who has shown the soul what it really is and all that God has pardoned it, would not instantly and most willingly forgive, and be at peace, and remain well-affected towards anyone who has injured her.

For the divine kindness and mercy shown her prove the immense love felt for her by the Almighty, and she is overjoyed at having an opportunity of showing love in return.

I repeat that I know a number of people whom our Lord has raised to supernatural things, giving them the prayer of contemplation I described, and though they have other faults and imperfections, I never saw one who was unforgiving, nor do I think it possible if these favours were from God.

God always enriches the souls he visits. This is certain, for although the favour and consolation may pass away quickly, it is detected later on by the benefits it has left in the soul.

Teresa of Avila

True peace

Two old men had lived together for many years and they had never fought with one another. The first said to the other, 'Let us also have a fight like other men.' The other replied, 'I do not know how to fight.' The first said to him, 'Look, I will put a  brick between us and I will say: it is mine; and you will reply: no, it is mine; and so the fight will begin.' So they put a brick between them and the first said, 'This brick is mine', and the other said, 'No, it is mine.' And the first replied, 'If it is yours, take it and go.' So they gave it up without being able to find a cause for an argument.

A brother asked abba Poemen, 'How should I behave in my cell in the place where I am living?' He replied, 'Behave as if you were a stranger, and wherever you are, do not expect your words to have any influence and you will be at peace.'

The Desert Fathers

Hearsay-religion and true faith

The reason why we know so little of Jesus Christ as our Saviour, why we are so destitute of that faith in him which alone can change, rectify and redeem our souls, why we live starving in the coldness and deadness of a formal, historical hearsay-religion, is this: we are strangers to our own inward misery and wants, we know not that we lie in the jaws of death and hell.

We keep all things quiet within us, partly by outward forms and modes of religion and morality, and partly by the comforts, cares and delights of this world. Hence it is that we believe in a Saviour not because we feel an absolute want of one, but because we have been told there is one, and that it would be a rebellion against God to reject him.

True faith is a coming to Jesus Christ to be saved and delivered from a sinful nature, as the Canaanite woman came to him and would not be denied. It is a faith that in love and longing and hunger and thirst and full assurance will lay hold on Christ as its loving, assured, certain and infallible Saviour.

It is this faith that breaks off all the bars and chains of death and hell in the soul; it is to this faith that Christ always says what he said in the gospel: 'Your faith has saved you, your sins are forgiven you; go in peace.'

William Law

The two deaths

As a man you are destined to die. Put it off as long as you like, the thing so long delayed will come at last.

There is, however, another death, from which the Lord came to deliver us: eternal death, the death of damnation with the devil and his angels. That is the real death; the other is only a change, the leaving of the body.

Do not fear this kind, but be frightened of the other, and labour to live in such a way that after death you may live with God.

Remember that Antichrists are not only to be found among those who have gone away from us, but among many who are still in the Church. The perjurer, the adulterer, the drunkard, the trafficker in drugs, all evil-doers.

They will say, 'But he made us like this'. Our Creator cries out from Heaven, 'I made the man, not the thief, the adulterer, the miser; all that moves in the sea, flies in the air, or walks on the earth is my work, and sings my praise'. But does avarice praise the Lord, or drunkenness, or impurity? Anything that does not praise him was not made by him.

Augustine

Sin cannot hinder love

Full lovingly does our Lord hold us when it seems to us we are nearly forsaken and cast away because of our sin – and deservedly so.

Our courteous Lord does not want his servants to despair even when they fall often and grievously into sin. For our falling does not hinder him from loving us.

This is princely friendship from our courteous Lord that he still sustains us secretly even while we are in sin. He touches us gently and shows us our sin by the kindly light of mercy and grace.

His will is that we should be like him in wholeness and never-ending love to ourselves and our fellow-Christians.

Julian of Norwich

God's action in the depths of the soul

The best way of dealing with idle thoughts is not to combat them and still less to be anxious and troubled about them, but just to let them drop like a stone into the sea. Gradually the habit of acting thus will become easy.

The second way to think only of God is to forget everything else, and one arrives at this state by dint of dropping all idle thoughts, so that it often happens that for some time one may pass whole days without, apparently, thinking of anything, as though one had become quite stupid.

It often happens that God even places certain souls in this state, which is called the emptiness of the spirit and of the understanding, or the state of nothingness.

The annihilation of one's own spirit wonderfully prepares the soul for the reception of that of Jesus Christ.

This is the mystical death to the working of one's own activity, and renders the soul capable of undergoing the divine operation.

Jean-Pierre de Caussade

The imitation of Christ

Pride is the great sin, the head and cause of all sins, and its beginning lies in turning away from God. Beloved, do not make light of this vice, for the proud man who disdains the yoke of Christ is constrained by the harsher yoke of sin: he may not wish to serve, but he has to, because if he will not be love's servant, he will inevitably be sin's slave.

From pride arises apostasy: the soul goes into darkness and misusing its free will falls into other sins, wasting its substance with harlots, and he who was created a fellow of the angels becomes a keeper of swine.

Because of this great sin of pride, God humbled himself, taking the nature of a servant, bearing insults and hanging on a cross. To heal us, he became humble; shall we not be ashamed to be proud?

You have heard the Lord say that if you forgive those who have injured you, your Father in heaven will forgive you. But those who speak the world's language say, 'What! you won't revenge yourself, but let him boast of what he did to you? Surely you will let him see that he is not dealing with a weakling?' Did the Lord revenge himself on those who struck him? Dying of his own free will, he uttered no threats: and will you, who do not know when you will die, get in a rage and threaten?

Augustine

The cross – true peace of mind

You do indeed 'seek peace and ensue it', but altogether in the wrong way. You seek the peace the
world gives, not the peace Christ gives.

Are you not aware, my dear father prior, how God
is so wonderful among his people that he has set his
peace where there is no peace, that is in the midst of
all our trials? As he says, 'Rule thou in the midst
of thine enemies'.

It is not, therefore, that man whom no one bothers
who has peace. That kind of peace is the peace the
world gives. It is that man whom everyone disturbs
and everyone harasses, and yet, who joyfully and
quietly endures them all.

You are saying with Israel, 'Peace! Peace!' when there
is no peace. Say, rather, with Christ, 'Cross! Cross!'
and there is no cross. For the cross ceases to be a
cross the moment you say gladly, 'Blessed cross! Of
all the trees that are in the wood there is none such
as thee!'

Seek this peace and you will find peace. Seek for
nothing else than to take on trials with joy. Seek
them as you would holy relics. You will never find
this peace by seeking and choosing what you feel and
judge to be the path of peace.

Martin Luther

The cross – a way of life

Therefore, my dear friar, learn Christ and him crucified. Learn to despair of your own efforts and learn to pray to him, learn to cry to him: 'Lord Jesus, thou art my righteousness, but I am thy sin. Thou hast taken upon thyself what is mine, and hast given me what is thine: thou hast taken upon thyself what thou wast not, and hast given me what I was not.'

Beware of aspiring to a righteousness of such purity that you would not wish to be looked upon as a sinner, or, still worse, not to be one! For Christ dwells only in sinners. It was for this very reason he descended from heaven, where he had his dwelling with the righteous, to dwell among us poor sinners on earth. Meditate on love of such power, and you will then experience his consolation of love.

Why did he have to die if we can of ourselves find a good conscience by means of our own works and self-imposed afflictions?

You will never find peace of mind except in Christ alone, and even then, only when you have despaired of yourself and of your own works.

You will also learn from him that just in the manner he has accepted you, so has he made your sins his own, and also his righteousness your own.

Martin Luther

The cross – in practice

The apostle teaches, Receive one another, as Christ also received us to the glory of God.* And again, Let this mind be in you which was also in Christ Jesus: who, though he was in the form of God, did not count equality with God a thing to be grasped, but emptied himself, taking the form of a servant . . . obedient unto . . . death on a cross.† In like manner, if you think of yourself as on a higher level of spirituality than they, do not reckon this righteousness as booty to be snatched at, as if it were your own, but humble yourself, forget what you are, and, after the fashion of Christ, be as one of them so that you can help them.

Pray for whatever you lack, kneeling before Christ. Christ will teach you all things. This one thing do: keep your eyes fixed on that which he has done for you and for all men so that you may learn what you should do for others. If Christ had sought to live only among nice people, and to die only for his friends, with whom would he have ever lived, for whom then would he have died? Go and do thou likewise, my dear friar, and continue to pray for me. The Lord be with you. Farewell in the Lord.

Martin Luther

* Rm 15:7.   † Ph 2:5ff.

73

Knowing God before loving him

[Brother Lawrence wrote]:

Our good Sister —— seems to me full of goodwill, but she wants to go faster than grace. One does not become holy all at once. I commend her to you.

I am filled with shame and confusion when I reflect, on the one hand, upon the great favours which God has bestowed and is still bestowing upon me; and, on the other, upon the ill use I have made of them, and my small advancement in the way of perfection.

We cannot escape the dangers which abound in life without the actual and continual help of God. Let us, then, pray to him for it continually. How can we pray to him without being with him? How can we be with him but in thinking of him often? And how can we often think of him unless by a holy habit of thought which we should form?

You will tell me that I am always saying the same thing. It is true, for this is the best and easiest method I know; and as I use no other, I advise all the world to do it.

We must know before we can love. In order to know God, we must often think of him; and when we come to love him we shall then also think of him often, for our heart will be with our treasure.

Brother Lawrence

74

God is our peace

The soul is immediately at one with God, when it is truly at peace in itself.

God is our sure rock, and he shall be our whole joy and make us as changeless as he is, when we reach the heavens.

When we come to receive the reward that grace has won for us, then we shall thank and bless our Lord, for ever rejoicing that we were called upon to suffer.

I saw full surely that wherever our Lord appears, peace reigns, and anger has no place. For I saw no whit of anger in God – in short or in long term.

It is God's will that we should serve him steadfastly for love, without grumbling or striving against him, until our life's end.

Julian of Norwich

The will of God and
the harmony of creation

God created everything to partake of his own nature, to have some degree and share of his own life and happiness. Nothing can be good or evil, happy or unhappy, but as it does or does not stand in the same degree of divine life in which it was created, receiving in God and from God all that good that it is capable of, and co-operating with him according to the nature of its powers and perfections.

As soon as it turns to itself and would, as it were, have a sound of its own, it breaks off from the divine harmony and falls into the misery of its own discord; and all its workings then are only so many sorts of torment or ways of feeling its own poverty.

The redemption of mankind can then only be effected, the harmony of the creation can then only berestored when the will of God is the will of every creature.

For this reason our blessed Lord, having taken upon him a created nature, so continually declares against the doing of anything of himself and always appeals to the will of God as the only motive and end of everything he did, saying that it was his meat and drink to do the will of him that sent him.

William Law

Christ's cross

Christ's cross over this face,
and thus over my ear.
Christ's cross over this eye.
Christ's cross over this nose.

Christ's cross to accompany
me before. Christ's cross to
accompany me behind me.
Christ's cross to meet every difficulty both on hollow
and hill.

Christ's cross eastwards facing me. Christ's cross
back towards the sunset. In the north, in the south,
increasingly may Christ's cross straightway be.

Christ's cross up to broad Heaven. Christ's cross
down to earth. Let no evil or hurt come to my body
or my soul.

Christ's cross over me as I sit. Christ's cross over me
as I lie. Christ's cross be all my strength until we
reach the King of Heaven.

From the top of my head to the nail of my foot, O
Christ, against every danger I trust in the protection
of the cross.

Till the day of my death, going into this clay, I shall
draw without – Christ's cross over this face.

The Celtic Tradition

The two commandments

Keep this always before you: that you are to love God and your neighbour. The love of God is the first to be commanded, but the love of your neighbour is the first to be fulfilled.

You cannot yet see God, but you earn the right to see him by loving your neighbour; and looking at the source of that love, you will see God as much as you can now.

Remember that in Christ you have everything. Do you want to love God? You have him in Christ. Do you want to love your neighbour? You have him in Christ, for 'the Word was made flesh'.

You know that the perfection of love is to love your enemy, but at least take great care that you do not hate your brother — if you love only your brother you are not perfect, but if you hate him where are you? What are you? Search your hearts.

Do not bear a grudge because of a harsh word, do not sink down to the level of the earth because of a quarrel over earthly things.

Do not imagine that if you hate your brother you live in Christ and walk in the light. 'The man who says he is in the light and yet hates his brother is still in the dark.'

Augustine

On care and calm in our affairs

The diligence and care with which we should attend to our affairs is very different from anxiety. Care and diligence are compatible with tranquillity and peace of mind; anxiety, over-carefulness and agitation are not.

Be careful and diligent in all your business, for God who has given it to you would want it done well. But avoid anxiety, do not hurry and excite yourself.

Nothing was ever done well that was done with haste and impetuosity. The old proverb is 'make haste slowly'. Try to meet the occupations facing you quietly, do them one after the other. If you try to do them all at once or in confusion, your spirit will be so overcharged and depressed that it will probably sink under the burden without achieving anything.

In all your undertakings rely wholly on God's providence, through which alone they can succeed. But steadily seek on your part to co-operate with it. Then be satisfied that if you are trusting all to God, whatever happens will be best for you, whether it seems to your judgement good or bad.

Francis de Sales

Facing an early death

It seems to me that nothing stands in the way of my going to heaven. I no longer have any great desires, beyond that of loving till I die of love. I am free, and I fear nothing, not even what I once dreaded more than anything else, a long illness which would make me a burden to the community.

Should it please God, I am quite content to have my sufferings of body and soul prolonged for years. I do not shrink from a long life: I do not refuse the battle. The Lord is the rock upon which I stand – 'who teaches my hands to fight, and my fingers to war. He is my protector and I have hoped in him' (Psalm 144:1–2).

I have never asked God to let me die young, but I have always thought that this favour will be granted me.

Very often God is satisfied with our wish to labour for his glory, and how immense are my desires to do so.

Thérèse of Lisieux

No condemnation

Since a believer need not come into condemnation, even though he be *surprised* into what his soul abhors (suppose his being surprised is not owing to any carelessness or wilful neglect of his own); if thou who believest art thus overtaken in a fault, then grieve unto the Lord: it shall be a precious balm.

Pour out thy heart before him, and show him of thy trouble; and pray with all thy might to him who is 'touched with the feeling of thy infirmities', that he would establish, and strengthen, and settle thy soul, and suffer thee to fall no more.

But still he condemneth thee not. Wherefore shouldst thou fear? Thou hast no need of any 'fear that hath torment'. Thou shalt love him that loveth thee, and it sufficeth: more love will bring more strength. And as soon as thou lovest him with all thy heart, thou shalt be 'perfect and entire, lacking nothing'.

Wait in peace for that hour when 'the God of peace shall sanctify thee wholly, so that thy whole spirit and soul and body may be preserved blameless unto the coming of our Lord Jesus Christ'.

John Wesley

The state of our will makes the state of our life

It is the state of our will that makes the state of our life; when we receive anything from God and do everything for God, everything does us the same good and helps us to the same degree of happiness.

Sickness and health, prosperity and adversity, bless and pacify such a soul in the same degree. As it turns everything towards God, so everything becomes divine to it. For he that seeks God in everything is sure to find God in everything.

When we thus live wholly unto God, God is wholly ours and we are happy in all that happiness of God. For in uniting with him in heart and will and spirit we are united to all that he is and has in himself.

This is the purity and perfection of life that we pray for in the Lord's Prayer, that God's Kingdom may come and his will be done in us as it is in heaven. And this, we may be sure, is not only necessary but attainable by us, or our Saviour would not have made it a part of our daily prayer.

William Law

Boldness in prayer

Sit in the presence of the Lord every moment of your life, as you think of him and recollect him in your heart.

Otherwise, when you only see him after a period of time, you will lack freedom of converse with him, out of shame; for great freedom of converse is born out of constant association with him.

Constant association with fellow-beings involves the body, whereas when it is with God, it involves the soul's meditation and the offering of prayers.

As a result of its great intensity, this meditation is sometimes mingled with wonder: 'The heart of those who seek the Lord shall rejoice' [see Psalm 105:3].

Seek the Lord, O sinners, and be strengthened in your thoughts with hope.

Seek his face through repentance at all times – and you shall be sanctified by the holiness of his face. You shall be purged clean of your wickedness.

Run to the Lord, all who are wicked; he forgives wickedness and removes sins.

Isaac of Syria

Not here, not here

There is only one thing you can be sure of: that you will die; everything else in this life, good or bad, is uncertain except death. Wherever you turn there is uncertainty; only death is sure, but even the day of your death is uncertain.

We are wanderers with no permanent home on earth; that is in heaven, and we do not know when we shall hear, 'Come, set out for home'. Only let us be ready. We shall be, if we long now for our true fatherland.

And yet only with difficulty, because of our weakness, can we unceasingly direct our hearts and works to God. We try to find something in this world to rest in, to pause and lie down. I do not mean the resting-places lovers of evil seek: foul amusements, cheating others, a life of luxury.

No – look at the good man: he seeks his whole refreshment in his family, in a humble life, in the house he has built for himself; these are the satisfactions of the innocent.

But our all-embracing love must be for eternal life, and so God allows bitterness to be mixed with these things. Don't be upset when these innocent pleasures have their trials; the man journeying to his own country must not mistake the inn for his home.

Augustine

God's handmaid

He brought our blessed Lady
to my mind. In my mind I
saw her as if she breathed – a
simple, humble girl, not
much more than a child; the
age she was when she
conceived. God showed me,
too, in part, the wisdom
and truth of her soul, so that
I understood the reverence

she felt before God her Maker and how she marvelled
that he would be born of her – a simple soul that he
himself had made. It was this wisdom and this truth
in her that showed her the greatness of her Maker
and the smallness of herself whom he had made. And
it was this that made her say so humbly to Gabriel,
'Behold God's handmaid.' By this I know surely that
she is higher in worth and grace than anyone that
God has made. For no one that is made is above her,
except the blessed humanity of Christ.

I trusted God's mercy.

Julian of Norwich

All consists in loving well

Endeavour to become humble and simple as a little child for the love of our Lord, in imitation of him, and in a spirit of peace and recollection. If God finds this humility in us he will prosper his work in us himself.

Persevere in being faithful to grace for the greater glory of God and for the pure love of him. All consists in loving well, and with all your heart and in all your employments, this God of all goodness.

When God grants us attractions and sensible devotion let us profit by them to attach ourselves more firmly to him above all his gifts.

But in times of dryness let us go on always in the same way, reminding ourselves of our poverty and also thinking that, perhaps, God wishes to prove our love for him by these salutary trials.

Let us be really humble, occupied in correcting our own faults, without reflecting on those of others.

Let us see Jesus Christ in all our neighbours, and then we shall have no difficulty in excusing them as well as helping them. Besides, we must bear with ourselves also out of charity.

Jean-Pierre de Caussade

Who can save us?

There are those who rely on their important friends or their own abilities, and others on their wealth – a presumption common to man. But do you really suppose that another man can save you from the wrath to come? The Psalmist says, 'his brother shall redeem him', but who is this brother? It is he who after his resurrection said, 'Go and tell my brothers'. When we call God our Father we are calling Christ our brother, and so need not fear the evil day, since we are not relying on ourselves or our powerful friends but on him who died for us so that we might not die an eternal death, who humbled himself that we might be raised up.

If Christ be not our redeemer, who can save us? For even if a man has led a holy life, it will go hard with him if you put aside your mercy when he stands before you. But you do not search out our sins in anger, and so we believe that one day our home will be with you. This is our hope, but let us know ourselves.

If we reckon up our deserts they are only a list of your gifts; and let us not say we have no debt to pay, in case the devil should prove us wrong, and take us to himself. Let us answer that our debt has been paid by Christ, that holy victim we receive at your altar, in whom we have triumphed over the enemy.

Augustine

For the love of Jesus

Be watchful of time and how you spend it. Nothing is more precious than time. In the twinkling of an eye heaven may be won or lost.

Time is made for man, not man for time.

I hear you say sadly, 'How shall I fare? And if what you say is true, how shall I give account of each moment of time? – I, who am now twenty-four, and until now have never paid heed to time . . . Help me now for the love of Jesus.'

That is indeed well said: 'For the love of Jesus'. For in the love of Jesus you shall find your help.

So then love Jesus, and all that he has is yours. Knit yourself to him by love and faith.

Author of 'The Cloud of Unknowing'

Freedom of spirit

The person who is detached from creatures is not disturbed during prayer or otherwise, and so, without losing precious time, he easily acquires heavenly treasure. On the other hand, the covetous man runs hither and thither within the limits of the chain binding his heart. Despite all efforts he can scarcely free himself even for a moment from the bondage of his thoughts, which run constantly to the place where he has fixed his heart.

The spiritual man must keep in mind that there is nothing a man can truly rejoice in except serving God, promoting his honour and glory, and directing all things to this end.

When a man is purged of all attachment to things the judgement is left clear as the sky when the mists have dispersed. His joy is not dependent on creatures, for while his heart is set on none of them he possesses them all.

John of the Cross

The book of all books

The book of all books is in your own heart, in which are written and engraven the deepest lessons of divine instruction; learn therefore to be deeply attentive to the presence of God in your hearts, who is always speaking, always instructing, always illuminating that heart that is attentive to him.

Here you will meet the divine light in its proper place, in that depth of your souls, where the birth of the Son of God and the proceeding of the Holy Ghost are always ready to spring up in you.

And be assured of this, that so much as you have of inward love and adherence to his holy light and spirit within you, so much as you have of real unaffected humility and meekness, so much as you are dead to your own will and self-love, so much as you have of purity of heart, so much, and no more, nor any further, do you see and know the truths of God.

William Law

Day by day

Dear sister, I see more need than ever to spend my remaining days in giving myself up daily and continually, body and soul, into the care of him who is able to keep that which is committed to him against that day. Not to give myself once, but to live continually giving myself, right up to and in the very moment when I put away this tabernacle. Dear sister, the thought of putting it away is particularly sweet sometimes; I can say that this is what cheers me more than anything else in these days, not death in itself, but the great gain that is to be got through it. To be able to leave behind every inclination that goes against the will of God, to leave behind every ability to dishonour the law of God, with all weakness swallowed up by strength, to become fully conformed to the law which is already on one's heart and to enjoy God's likeness for ever. Dear sister, I am sometimes absorbed so far into these things that I completely fail to stand in the way of my duty with regard to temporal things, but I look for the time when I may find release and be with Christ, for that is much better, although it is very good here through a lattice, and the Lord sometimes reveals through a glass, darkly, as much of his glory as my weak faculties can bear.

The Celtic Tradition

Seeking with faith, hope and love

And this showing [the second] was to teach me that when the soul continually seeks God, it pleases him greatly. For the soul can do no more than seek, suffer and trust, and this is the work of the Holy Spirit in the soul. And the clearness in finding him comes by his special grace, when it is his will.

This seeking with faith, hope and love pleases our Lord, and the finding pleases the soul and fills it full of joy.

And so I was taught in my mind that seeking is as good as seeing during the time he lets the soul labour. It is God's will that we seek after him to see him, so that he can show himself to us by his special grace, when it is his will.

And he himself shall teach a soul how it may come to have a sight of him. And this is most glory to him and profit to you, and the richest way to receive meekness and virtue by the guidance of the Holy Ghost. For a soul that entirely clings to him with true trust, either of seeking or seeing, brings the highest worship it can to him, as I see it.

Julian of Norwich

Three qualities in our seeking

There are two works that can be seen in this showing; one is seeking, the other is seeing.

The seeking is commonplace – that is, every soul can undertake it by his grace, and ought to do so by the direction and teaching of Holy Church.

It is God's will that we have three things in our seeking.

The first is that we seek willingly and actively, without sloth, as we can through his grace, gladly and happily, without foolish gladness and empty sorrow.

The second is that we wait on him steadfastly for love, not grumbling and striving against him, until our life's end – for it lasts so short a time.

The third is that we trust him completely with certainty of faith, because this is his will.

We know he will come suddenly and joyfully to all who love him. For his way is secret, his way is to be seen, his coming shall be right sudden, and his will is to be trusted – for he is gracious and homely. Blessed may he be!

Julian of Norwich

Desire for and attachment to riches

No one will admit to being avaricious. We excuse ourselves on the plea of providing for our children, or on that of prudence and forethought. We never have too much, but always find a good reason for seeking more. Even the greatest misers will not confess their avarice, and in their own conscience do not believe themselves to be avaricious.

If you desire eagerly and anxiously that which you do not have, though you may say you do not seek to acquire it unjustly, you are still really avaricious.

I doubt if it is possible to desire to possess honestly that which another possesses, for by this desire we must involve the other's loss. Do not give way to the wish for that which is another's until he on his part wishes to part with it; then his desire will make you not only just but charitable. I would not forbid you to extend your means and possessions so long as you do it not only with justice but with gentleness and charity. But do not fix your heart on that which you have, and do not be overpowered by any losses with which you meet.

Francis de Sales

Real poverty when actually rich

You should be much more watchful than men of the world are, in order to turn your possessions to good use. Our possessions are not our own. God has given them to us so that we may cultivate them, and it is his will that we should make them useful and fruitful, so rendering him an acceptable service.

Self-love is violent, turbulent and restive, so that our cares on its behalf will be troubled, anxious and uneasy. The love of God is gentle, peaceful and tranquil, so that our cares springing from that source, although they concern worldly goods, will be gentle, mild and without anxiety.

However, it is as well to practise real practical poverty in the midst of the riches and advantages with which God has endowed you. Always dispose part of your means by giving alms freely to the poor, for you impoverish yourself of that which you give, and the more it is, the more you are impoverished.

Love poverty and the poor; for by this you will become truly poor yourself, since we become like that which we love.

Francis de Sales

Watering the garden of the soul

Let us see how this garden is
to be watered, that we may
understand what we have to
do: how much trouble it will
cost us, whether the gain be
greater than the trouble, or
how long it will take us.

It seems to me that the garden
may be watered in four ways: by water taken out of
a well, which is very laborious; or with water raised
by a water-wheel and buckets, drawn by a windlass
– I have drawn it this way sometimes – it is a less
troublesome way than the first, and gives more
water; or by a stream or brook, whereby the garden
is watered in a much better way – for the soil is more
thoroughly saturated, and there is no necessity to
water it so often, and the labour of the gardener is
much less; or by showers of rain, when our Lord
himself waters it, without labour on our part – and
this way is incomparably better than all the others of
which I have spoken.

I hope, by the help of this comparison, to explain
the four degrees of prayer to which our Lord, of his
goodness, has occasionally raised my soul.

Teresa of Avila

Beginning

Of those who are beginners in prayer, we may say that they are those who draw the water up out of the well – a process which, as I have said, is very laborious; for they must be wearied in keeping the senses recollected, and this is a great labour, because the senses have been hitherto accustomed to distractions.

It is necessary for beginners to accustom themselves to disregard what they hear or see, and to put it away from them during the time of prayer; they must be alone, and in retirement think over their past life.

Beginners at first suffer much, because they are not convinced that they are penitent for their sins; and yet they are, because they are so sincerely resolved on serving God.

They must strive to meditate on the life of Christ, and the understanding is wearied thereby.

Thus far we can advance of ourselves – that is, by the grace of God – for without that, as everyone knows, we never can have one good thought.

Teresa of Avila

Second degree of prayer

Let us now speak of the second manner of drawing water, which the Lord of the vineyard has ordained; of the machine of wheel and buckets whereby the gardener may draw more water with less labour, and be able to take some rest without being continually at work. I apply this to the prayer called the prayer of quiet.

Herein the soul begins to be recollected; it is now touching on the supernatural – for it never could by any efforts of its own attain to this.

This is a gathering together of the faculties of the soul within itself, but the faculties are not lost, neither are they asleep; the will alone is occupied in such a way that, without knowing how it has become a captive, it gives a simple consent to become the prisoner of God; for it knows well what it is to be the captive of him it loves.

O my Jesus and my Lord, how pressing now is thy love! It binds our love in bonds so straitly, that it is not in its power at this moment to love anything else but thee.

Teresa of Avila

A spark of true love

The prayer of quiet, then, is a little spark of the true love of himself, which our Lord begins to enkindle in the soul; and his will is that the soul should understand what this love is by the joy it brings.

This spark given of God, however slight it may be, causes a great crackling; if men do not quench it by their faults, it is the beginning of a great fire, which sends forth the flames of that most vehement love of God which His Majesty will have perfect souls possess.

What the soul has to do is nothing more than to be gentle and without noise. By noise, I mean going about with the understanding in search of words and reflections whereby to give God thanks for his grace, and heaping up its sins and imperfections together to show that it does not deserve it.

Let it simply say words of love that suggest themselves now, firmly grounded in the conviction that what it says is truth.

Teresa of Avila

Christ in us the hope of glory

A Christ not in us is the same thing as a Christ not ours. If we are only so far with Christ as to own and receive the history of his birth, person and character, if this is all that we have of him, we are as much without him, as much left to ourselves, as little helped by him as those evil spirits which cried out 'we know thee, who thou art, thou holy one of God'.

It is the language of Scripture that Christ in us is our hope of glory, that Christ formed in us, growing and raising his own life and spirit in us, is our only salvation. For since the serpent, sin, death and hell are all essentially within us, the very growth of our nature, must not our redemption be equally inward, an inward essential death to this state of our souls, and an inward growth of a contrary life within us?

William Law

The hiddenness of the Holy Spirit's work

You have only to go on in the same way; but you explain yourself in a manner that might be misunderstood by those who have no experience of your state of prayer. You say that you do nothing; yet you must all the time be at work, otherwise your state would be one of mere laziness.

But your soul acts so quietly that you do not perceive your own interior acts of assent and adhesion to the impressions of the Holy Spirit.

The stronger these impressions are, the less is it necessary to act; you must only follow your attraction and allow yourself to be led quite calmly, as you so well express it.

Your way of acting in times of trouble and distress gives me great pleasure. To be submissive, to abandon yourself entirely without reserve, to be content with being discontented for as long as God wills or permits, will make you advance more in one day than you would in a hundred days spent in sweetness and consolation.

Your total abandonment to God, practised in a spirit of confidence, and of union with Jesus Christ doing always the will of his Father, is, of all practices, the most divine.

Jean-Pierre de Caussade

A sacrifice

What sacrifice can I offer to God that is worthy of his mercy? Shall I look for a victim from among my herds? No, I will freely offer a sacrifice of praise. Freely: for his sake alone, not for any other reason.

If you praise him for anything else, you do not praise him freely. Understand what I mean: suppose you praise God so that he may make you rich. If your riches could be acquired any other way, you would not praise him. By all means ask him for what will profit you for all eternity, but love and praise him for himself alone. 'Praise his name for he is good' – not for any other reason.

Remember God does not ask of us anything he has not already given us. He does not say, 'Look at your fields and herds and see what you can offer me as a holocaust.'

A holocaust is an offering wholly consumed by fire, and love itself is a blazing fire. When the soul is on fire with the love of God it draws the whole man to its purpose, leaving no room for lesser loves.

If you want to offer him the holocaust of which he has said, 'It is ever before my eyes', be ablaze with divine love, thanking him for giving you whatever is good in you and for forgiving you whatever is evil.

Augustine

The devil is scorned

In God there can be no anger, as I see it. For our good Lord always has in his mind his own goodness and the rewarding of all who shall be saved. He sets his might and his right in the path of the Evil One who, for wickedness and malice, busies himself to plot and work against God's will. Also, I saw our Lord scorn the devil's malice and expose his lack of power, and he wills that we should do so, too.

Because I saw this sight I laughed aloud and made those who were round me laugh too, and their laughing rejoiced my heart. I wanted all my fellow-Christians to see what I saw, so they would all laugh with me.

But I did not see Christ laugh, although I understood that we may laugh aloud in comforting ourselves and rejoicing in God because the devil is overcome.

I thought of Judgement Day and of all those who shall be saved, whose happiness he greatly envies. For at that day he shall see that all the grief and trouble he has brought upon them shall be turned into even greater joy for them, without end, and all the pain and tribulation he wished upon them shall go with him to hell, without end also.

Julian of Norwich

Prayer

They asked abba Macarius, 'How should we pray?'
And the old man replied, 'There is no need to speak
much in prayer; often stretch out your hands and
say, "Lord, as you will and as you know, have mercy
on me." But if there is war in your soul, add, "Help
me!" and because he knows what we need, he shows
mercy on us.'

Abba Lot went to see abba Joseph and he said to
him, 'Abba, as far as I can, I say my little office, I
fast a little, I pray and meditate, I live in peace and
as far as I can I purify my thoughts. What else can I
do?' Then the old man stood up and stretched his
hands towards heaven; his fingers became like ten
lamps of fire and he said to him, 'If you will, you
can become all flame.'

Abba Paul said, 'Keep close to Jesus.'

The Desert Fathers

The thankful heart

He who hath this hope [in Christ], thus 'full of immortality, in everything giveth thanks' as knowing that this (whatsoever it is) 'is the will of God in Christ Jesus concerning him'. From him, therefore, he cheerfully receives all, saying, 'Good is the will of the Lord', and whether the Lord giveth or taketh away, equally 'blessing the name of the Lord'. For he hath 'learned in whatsoever state he is, therewith to be content'.

Whether in ease or pain, whether in sickness or health, whether in life or death, he giveth thanks from the ground of his heart to him who orders it for good; knowing that, as 'every good gift cometh from above', so none but good can come from the Father of lights, into whose hand he has wholly committed his body and soul as into the hands of a faithful Creator.

He is therefore 'careful' [anxious or uneasy] 'for nothing', as having 'cast all his care on him that careth for him' and 'in all things' resting on him, after 'making his request known to him with thanksgiving'.

John Wesley

Fruits of the spirit

Create and multiply, means to increase the fruits of the spirit which are love, joy, peace, patience, kindness, goodness, trustfulness, gentleness and self-control (Galatians 5:22).

Praised be the Lord for giving me the grace to bear malicious gossip patiently.

In my heart I heard Jesus say:

'My grace is my special gift which I give to my chosen souls whom I know will live with me for ever.'

'While your thoughts are on me you cannot sin.'

Margery Kempe

Angharad

For many was her concern
At nightfall, and she rejoiced with many too,
Sensing the pain, joining the feast,
In the ocean of her heart was cherishing.
To her doors the troubled came
The weary knew the way to her court.
Angharad wore a scarlet gown
Down to her feet; it was made of good works.

She bore the turmoil of the fragile heart
Through her encouragement overcoming fears.
On her knees in the early morning
She gave her day to the Kingdom.
Giving the simplicity of her today
As wine to the King, and to the wound.
Caring for his riches
She recreated with her praise an unblemished
    world . . .

Anger and jealousy she broke
Healing with fruits of her tree;
Freely extending the generous gift . . .
She gave to God from the two aspects
Pain and joy in harmony.
She gives to us in the Spirit of the Lord
The priesthood of her concern.

The Celtic Tradition

Sin

In the sins instanced in the Ten Commandments we see nothing else but self-love, which seeks its own interests, takes from God what is his, from men what is theirs, and from all it is, has and does, gives nothing back to God or man. St Augustine well says, 'The beginning of all sin is the love of one's own self . . .' Therefore, he lives best who lives not for himself, and he who lives for himself, lives worst.

Be a sinner, and sin boldly; but more boldly still, believe in Christ and rejoice in him, for he is victorious over sin, death and the world. As long as we live in this world we are bound to sin . . . but no sin will separate us from Christ. Pray boldly – for you, too, are a mighty sinner.*

If you have the presumption to try to quiet your conscience with your own contrition and penitence, you will never come to peace of mind, but will, rather, end up in despair. If we allow sin to remain in our conscience and try to deal with it there, or if we look at sin in our heart, it will prove much too strong for us, and will remain for ever. But, if we look at it as borne by Christ, and see it overcome in his resurrection, and have the courage to believe this, it is in that very act dead. Sin cannot remain in Christ, for it is swallowed up in his resurrection.

Martin Luther

* Luther is, of course, not exhorting to sin but to faith and action in faith, even if, as a sinner, his good deeds are tainted with sin.

Love renders our task easy

[Brother Lawrence said]:

That all things are possible to him who believes.

They are less difficult to him who hopes.

They are more easy to him who loves, and still more easy to him who perseveres in the practice of these three virtues.

The end we ought to propose to ourselves is to become, in this life, the most perfect worshippers of God we can possibly be, as we hope to be through all eternity.

The greater perfection a soul aspires after, the more dependent it is upon divine grace.

Brother Lawrence

Loving others purely

When our hearts are free
from liking and judging
people merely according to
their natural gifts, we are not
held captive by external and
changing charms. We are
instead free to love people as
they really are, and we can
penetrate more easily to the
core of their personality, their true goodness.

When we love in this way our love is selfless and
pleasing to God.

The more this kind of love grows the more our love
of God grows with it; and the deeper our love for
him the more we shall love our neighbour for the
principle of both is the same.

A great benefit of this way of loving people is that
it fosters a large-hearted spirit, which is as necessary
in God's service as is interior freedom. With it temptations against love are easily overcome, we are able
to endure all things peacefully, and the virtues grow
and flourish within us.

John of the Cross

The glory of God

There are many Christians who are virtuous men, and who do great things, but their virtues and good works are utterly useless in the matter of eternal life, because they seek themselves in them, and not solely the honour and glory of God.

The Christian must keep in mind that the value of his good works depends on the love which motivates him to perform them for God. Those works are most perfect when wrought in the most sincere love of God, and with the least regard to present or future self-interest, joy and sweetness, consolation and praise.

The heart therefore must not rest in the joy, comfort, delight and advantages which holy habits and good works bring with them. It must refer all to God, desiring only that God may rejoice in what is done in secret, and with God's honour and glory as its only motivation.

Thus all the strength of the will will be concentrated on God.

John of the Cross

The power of prayer

The power of prayer is indeed wonderful. It is like a queen, who, having free access always to the king, can obtain whatever she asks. To secure a hearing there is no need to recite set prayers composed for the occasion – were this the case, I should indeed deserve to be pitied!

Apart from the Office [the daily prayer of the Church] which is a daily joy, I do not have the courage to search through books for beautiful prayers. They are so numerous that it would only make my head ache. Unable either to say them all or to choose between them, I do as a child would who cannot read – I just say what I want to say to God, quite simply, and he never fails to understand.

For me, prayer is an uplifting of the heart, a glance towards heaven, a cry of gratitude and love in times of sorrow as well as joy. It is something noble, something supernatural, which expands the soul and unites it to God.

When my state of spiritual aridity is such that not a single good thought will come, I repeat very slowly the Our Father and the Hail Mary, which are enough to console me, and provide food for my soul.

Thérèse of Lisieux

A child of God

This it is, in the judgement of the Spirit of God, to be a son or a child of God; it is, so to *believe* in God, through Christ, as 'not to commit sin', and to enjoy at all times, and in all places, that 'peace of God which passeth all understanding'.

It is, so to *hope* in God through the Son of his love, as to have not only the 'testimony of a good conscience', but also the Spirit of God 'bearing witness with your spirits, that you are the children of God'; whence cannot but spring the rejoicing evermore in him through whom you 'have received the atonement'.

It is, so to *love* God who hath thus loved you, as you never did love any creature: so that you are constrained to love all men as yourselves with a love not only ever burning in your hearts, but flaming out in all your actions and conversations, and making your whole life one 'labour of love', one continued obedience to those commands, 'Be you merciful, as God is merciful'; 'Be you holy, as I the Lord am holy'; 'Be you perfect, as your Father which is in heaven is perfect.'

John Wesley

The new commandment

The Lord said, 'I give you a new commandment: love one another as I have loved you.' By keeping this commandment sin is destroyed; not to love is not only deadly sin but the root of all other sin.

Let no one who does not love his brother think that he is a son of God; and when we look at our sins let us remember that 'love covers a multitude of sins'.

The perfection of love is to be willing to lay down one's life for one's brother, following the Lord's example who died for all men. But does love reach that height all at once? No – when it is born it needs to be nourished, nourished it becomes strong, and strengthened it becomes perfect.

No matter what you have, without love it is worthless; and if you love, nothing is lacking. 'The man who loves his brother has fulfilled the law.'

Don't imagine that you will be forgiven if you don't wholeheartedly forgive.

It is only human to be angry, but the feeble shoot of your anger must not be watered by suspicion and become a bough of hatred. The man who hates his brother is a murderer, and you know that a murderer's heart is empty of eternal life.

Augustine

Clothed with humility

Suppose God has now thoroughly cleansed our heart and scattered the last remains of sin; yet how can we be sensible enough of our own helplessness, our utter inability to all good, unless we are every hour, yea, every moment, 'endued with power from on high'?

We have need, even in this state of grace, to be thoroughly and continually penetrated with a sense of this. Otherwise we shall be in perpetual danger of robbing God of his honour by glorying in something we have received as though we had not received it.

When our inmost soul is thoroughly tinctured therewith, it remains that we be 'clothed with humility'. The word used by St Peter seems to imply that we be covered with it as with a surtout,* that we be all humility, both within and without; tincturing all we think, speak and do.

Let all our actions spring from this fountain; let all our words breathe this spirit; that all men may know we have been with Jesus and have learned of him to be lowly in heart.

John Wesley

* Overcoat.

Joy

Lord, you are my joy and happiness, the only treasure I have in this world. I do not wish for material goods but think only of you. My dear Lord and my God, do not leave me.

'Rejoice and be happy! If you knew how much pleasure I get from speaking to you, you would never do anything else.'

'If you said the Lord's Prayer a thousand times a day, it would not make me as glad as when you remain silent and let me speak to you.'

'You can be as sure of the love of God, as God is God. Your soul is more secure in the love of God than in your own body. Your soul will leave your body but God will never leave your soul.'

Margery Kempe

Neighbours

My brothers, do not think you must speak the truth to a Christian but can lie to a pagan. You are speaking to your brother, born like you from Adam and Eve: realize that each man is your neighbour even before he is a Christian; you have no idea how God sees him.

The man you mock at for adoring stones may be converted, and may worship God more fervently than you who laughed at him. Some who are not yet in the Church are near to us, and some hidden there are far away. You cannot see into the future, so let every man be your neighbour.

Suppose you saw someone walking in the dark and you knew of an open well into which he might fall and didn't warn him – you would rightly be held an enemy of his soul. And yet, if he fell in, only his body would die. If you see him falling into sin, and you chuckle over it – what then?

It is by love alone that the sons of God are distinguished from the children of the devil. A man can be baptized and so reborn but let him look into his heart and see if he loves his neighbour, and if so he can say truly, 'I am a child of God'. But if not, though he has received the character of the sacrament, he is no better than a deserter or a vagabond. Only those who love their brethren are children of God.

Augustine

Action, a way of prayer

[Brother Lawrence said]:

That the most excellent method he had found of going to God was that of doing our common business (for him received under obedience) without any view of pleasing men, and (as far as possible) purely for the love of God.

It was a great delusion to think that the times of prayer ought to differ from other times.

We are as strictly obliged to adhere to God by action in the time of action as by prayer in the season of prayer.

His view of prayer was nothing else but a sense of the presence of God, his soul being at that time insensible to everything but divine love.

When the appointed times of prayer were past, he found no difference because he still continued with God, praising him and blessing him with all his might, so that he passed his life in continual joy.

Even so, he hoped that God would give him something to suffer when he should have grown stronger.

Brother Lawrence

Joy in believing

Christ is a God of joy . . . A Christian should be and must be a man of joy.

The devil is the spirit of sadness, but God is the Spirit of joy, and he is our salvation.

We have more occasion for joy than sadness. The reason is we believe in the living God, and Christ lives, and we shall live also.

God can make himself known only through those works of his which he reveals in us, which we feel and experience within ourselves. When the experience is to learn that he is a God who looks into the depths and helps principally the poor, despised, afflicted, miserable, forsaken and those who are of no account, at that very moment a love for him is created and surges up from the heart's core. The heart overflows with gladness, and leaps and dances for the joy it has found in God.

In this experience the Holy Spirit is active, and has taught us in the flash of a moment the deep secret of joy.

You will have as much joy and laughter in life as you have faith in God.

Martin Luther

A Christian woman

'Think of your mother,' said he. 'Did you ever meet anyone who knew so much suffering? And yet did anyone enjoy more true happiness? Where did it spring from? From looking into herself? Not a bit of it! She had learnt to look on One who is worth looking at. I always felt that the greater her trials, the greater was her joy. Her poverty only made her mind dwell on the riches which are in Christ . . . Don't take offence, now, but the fact is that whenever I heard that your mother was in trouble, I would laugh and say, "Well, this is another feast for Mary Lewis!" . . . Never in my life did I see anyone who could live so completely as she could on the resources of her religion.'

The Celtic Tradition

When discouraged, trust in God's mercy

Beware, daughters, of a certain kind of humility suggested by the devil which is accompanied by great anxiety about the gravity of our sins.

He disturbs souls in many ways by this means, until at last he stops them from receiving Holy Communion and from private prayer by doubts as to whether they are in a fit state for it, and such thoughts as: 'Am I worthy of it? Am I in a good disposition? I am unfit to live in a religious community.'

Thus Christians are hindered from prayer, and when they communicate, the time during which they ought to be obtaining graces is spent in wondering whether they are well prepared or no.

Everything such a person says seems to her on the verge of evil, and all her actions appear fruitless, however good they are in themselves. She becomes discouraged and unable to do any good, for what is right in others she fancies is wrong in herself.

When you are in this state, turn your mind so far as you can from your misery and fix it on the mercy of God, his love for us, and all that he suffered for our sake.

Teresa of Avila

Work

God works in us and we work together with him; through us he preaches, has pity on the poor, and comforts the broken-hearted . . . God himself milks the cows through him whose job it is to milk cows!

God does not consider how small or large the works are, but looks on the heart, which performs in faith and obedience to what its calling demands.

It is God's clear intention that all Christians are to live in the same faith, and be moved and guided by the same Spirit; but in external matters to carry out different works.

No one is poor among Christians. If you do not have as much as the burgomaster, do you not rather have God the Creator of heaven and earth? And Christ? And prayer? The emperor does not have more!

Work, and let God give the fruits thereof!
Govern, and let him prosper your rule!
Battle, and let him yield the victory!
Preach, and let him make hearts devout!
Marry, and let him give you children!
Eat and drink, and let him give you health and
    strength!
Then it will follow, that whatever we do, he will
    effect everything through us. And to him alone
    shall be the glory!

Martin Luther

God with us

My mind and my heart gradually became so joined to God that he was continually with me in everything that lived. The more my love grew, the more I became aware of my own sins and my dependence upon God.

Lying in my bed I heard the Lord call my name. I listened in silence until he spoke.

'Where God is, heaven is. God is in your soul night and day.'

'When you go to church I go with you; when you sit down for a meal I sit with you; when you lie down to sleep I lie with you and when you go out I go with you.'

Margery Kempe

An Easter sermon

O death, where is thy sting? O grave, where is thy victory? This is so true that even Satan cannot deny it. Christ's resurrection and victory over sin, death and hell is greater than all heaven and earth. You can never imagine his resurrection and victory so great but that in actuality it is far, far greater. For as his person is mighty, eternal, without limit, incomprehensible, so also is his resurrection, victory and triumph mighty, eternal, without limit, incomprehensible. Were hell a thousand times more, and death ten thousand times more, it would all be but a spark, a mere drop, compared with Christ's resurrection, victory and triumph. But, his resurrection, victory and triumph gives Christ to all who believe in him. Since we have been baptized in his name, and believe in him, it follows that even if you and I underwent sin, death and hell a hundred thousandfold, it would amount to nothing; for Christ's resurrection, victory and triumph, which have been given me in the baptism and in the word by faith, and therefore are my own, are infinitely greater. If this is true, and I most certainly believe it to be true, then let sin, death and hell dog my steps and growl at me. What will they do to us? What can they do? What?

Martin Luther

The road home

And so, brethren, in this life we are pilgrims; we sigh in faith for our true country which we are unsure about. Why do we not know the country whose citizens we are? Because we have wandered so far away that we have forgotten it. But the Lord Christ, the king of that land, came down to us, and drove forgetfulness from our heart. God took to himself our flesh so that he might be our way back. We go forward through his Manhood so that we may be with him for ever in his Godhead. Do not look for any path to him except himself; for if he had not vouchsafed to be the way, we could never have found the path. I do not tell you to look for the way – the way has come to you: arise and walk.

You are not walking on the lake like Peter, but on another sea, for this world is a sea: trials its waves, temptations its storms, and men devouring each other as fishes do. Don't be afraid, step out stoutly lest you sink. Peter said, 'If it is you, bid me come to you on the water.' It was, and he heard his cry and raised him as he was sinking. Gaze in faith at this miracle, and do as Peter did. When the gale blows and the waves rise, and your weakness makes you fear you will be lost, cry out, 'Lord, I am sinking', and he who bade you walk will not let you perish.

Augustine

The daily life – a pilgrimage to heaven

This life is not a state of being righteous, but
rather, of growth in righteousness;

not a state of being healthy,
but a period of healing;

not a state of being,
but becoming;

not a state of rest,
but of exercise and activity.

We are not yet what we shall be,
but we grow towards it;

the process is not yet finished,
but is still going on;

this life is not the end,
it is the way to a better.

All does not yet shine with glory;
nevertheless, all is being purified.*

Martin Luther

* 2 Co 3:18.

Love to all

Seeing thou canst do all things through Christ strengthening thee, be merciful as thy Father in heaven is merciful. Love thy neighbour as thyself. Love friends and enemies as thine own soul; and let thy love be long-suffering and patient towards all men.

Let it be kind, soft, benign; inspiring thee with the most amiable sweetness, and the most fervent and tender affection. Let it rejoice in the truth whereso-ever it is found; the truth that is after godliness. Enjoy whatever brings glory to God, and promotes peace and goodwill among men.

In love, cover all things. Of the dead and the absent speak nothing but good. Believe all things which may in any way tend to clear your neighbour's character. Hope all things in his favour and endure all things, triumphing over all opposition: for true love never faileth, in time or in eternity.

John Wesley

The mercy of God

As a handful of sand thrown into the ocean, so are the sins of all flesh as compared with the mind of God.

Just as a strongly flowing fountain is not blocked up by a handful of earth, so the compassion of the Creator is not overcome by the wickedness of his creatures.

Someone who bears a grudge while he prays is like a person who sows in the sea and expects to reap a harvest.

As the flame of a fire cannot be prevented from ascending upwards, so the prayers of the compassionate cannot be held back from ascending to heaven.

Isaac of Syria

He keeps all that is made

He showed me a little thing, the size of a hazelnut, in the palm of my hand, and it was as round as a ball. I looked at it with my mind's eye and I thought, 'What can this be?' And answer came, 'It is all that is made.' I marvelled that it could last, for I thought it might have crumbled to nothing, it was so small. And the answer came into my mind, 'It lasts and ever shall because God loves it.' And all things have being through the love of God.

In this little thing I saw three truths. The first is that God made it. The second is that God loves it. The third is that God looks after it.

What is he indeed that is Maker and Lover and Keeper? I cannot find words to tell. For until I am one with him I can never have true rest nor peace. I can never know it until I am held so close to him that there is nothing in between.

For he is endless and has made us for his own self only, and has restored us by his blessed Passion, and keeps us in his blessed love. And he does all this through his goodness.

God, of your goodness, give me yourself, for you are enough for me.

Julian of Norwich

God is our true peace

So I saw that God is our true peace. He watches over us when we can find no rest, and he works continually to bring us to peace that shall never end.

And when, through the power of mercy and grace, we are made humble and gentle, we are wholly safe. Then suddenly the soul is at one with God, when it is truly at peace with itself, for no anger is found in him.

And so I saw that, when we are full of peace and love, we find no striving in ourselves and are not hindered by the strife that is in us now. For that strife is the cause of our troubles and all our sorrow.

And our Lord takes our strivings and sends them up to heaven where they are made more sweet and delectable than heart can think, or tongue can tell.

And when we get there we shall find them waiting, all turned into lovely and lasting glory.

So God is our sure rock, and he shall be our whole joy, and make us changeless as he is, when we reach heaven.

Julian of Norwich

Humility and peace

No one has understanding if he is not humble, and he who lacks humility is devoid of understanding.

No one is humble if he is not at peace, and he who is not at peace is not humble. And no one is at peace without rejoicing.

In all the paths on which people journey in this world they will find no peace until they draw near to the hope which is God.

The heart finds no peace from toil and from stumbling-blocks until it is brought close to hope – which makes it peaceful and pours joy into it.

This is what the venerable and holy lips of our Lord said: 'Come unto me all who are weary and heavy laden, and I will give you rest.'*

Draw near, he says, to hope in me; desist from the many ways and you will find rest from labour and fear.'

Isaac of Syria

* Mt 11:28.

131

Love

Lord, I am here because I
love you; help me and show
me what to do.

In my heart I heard Jesus say,
'Love me as I love you. I
have chosen you and keep
continual watch over you.
You cannot solve all your
problems without my help.'

'I am within you and you are within me; if people
listen to you they will hear my voice. When people
are kind to you they are kind to me but if they are
unkind to you, then they are unkind to me.'

Margery Kempe

The opinion of others – God's purpose

I cannot say God makes me walk in the way of exterior humiliation; he is content with humbling me in my inmost soul. In the eyes of creatures, success crowns all my efforts – I seem to walk the dangerous path of honour. In this respect, I understand the design of God.

If I were looked upon as a useless member of the community, incapable and wanting in judgement, I would not be asked to help others. And so the Lord has thrown a veil over my shortcomings, interior and exterior. Sincere compliments come to me, but the remembrance of my weakness is so constantly present to me that there is no room for vanity.

However, I tire at times of this oversweet food and long for something other than praise. Then the Lord serves me a salad, well-flavoured and mixed with plenty of vinegar, and without oil. At the moment I least expect it, this salad is set before me.

Lifting the veil that hides my faults, God allows people to see me as I really am, and they tell me quite simply how I try them and what they dislike in me. Strangely, this salad pleases me and fills my soul with joy. How can something so contrary to nature afford joy? Had I not experienced it I would not have believed it possible.

Thérèse of Lisieux

The fact of self-deception

Let us now come to the time of trial – for we can only test ourselves by watching our actions narrowly, and we shall soon detect signs of deceptions.

For instance, as regards humility. We fancy we do not wish for honour and that we are indifferent to everything of the kind – yet let anyone offer us the slightest affront, and our feelings and behaviour will at once betray that we are not humble.

Besides, if any opportunity occurs of augmenting our dignity we do not reject it for the sake of a greater good. And God grant we may not seek such honour.

We are so accustomed to saying that we want nothing and are indifferent to everything (which we really believe is the fact), that at last the very habit of asserting it convinces us of its truth more strongly.

It is wise to be aware that this is a temptation, for when God gives us any solid virtue it brings all the others in its train.

Teresa of Avila

The prayer of the heart

All outward power that we exercise in the things about us is but as a shadow in comparison of that inward power that resides in our will, imagination and desires. These communicate with eternity and kindle a life which always reaches either heaven or hell.

Our desire is not only thus powerful and productive of real effects, but it is always alive, always working and creating in us – I say creating, for it has no less power, it perpetually generates either life or death in us.

And here lies the ground of the great efficacy of prayer, which, when it is the prayer of the heart, the prayer of faith, has a kindling and creating power, and forms and transforms the soul into everything that its desires reach after.

It has the key to the Kingdom of heaven and unlocks all its treasures, it opens, extends and moves that in us which has its being and motion in and with the divine nature, and so brings us into real union and communion with God.

William Law

Joy

When abba Apollo heard the sound of singing from the monks who welcomed us, he greeted us according to the custom which all monks follow . . . he first lay prostrate on the ground, then got up and kissed us and having brought us in he prayed for us; then, after washing our feet with his own hands, he invited us to partake of some refreshment . . .

One could see his monks were filled with joy and a bodily contentment such as one cannot see on earth. For nobody among them was gloomy or downcast.

If anyone did appear a little downcast, abba Apollo at once asked him the reason and told each one what was in the secret recesses of his heart. He used to say, 'Those who are going to inherit the Kingdom of heaven must not be despondent about their salvation . . . we who have been considered worthy of so great a hope, how shall we not rejoice without ceasing, since the Apostle urges us always, "Pray without ceasing, in everything give thanks"?'

The Desert Fathers

'Draw me', and we will run

One day after Holy Communion, the Lord made me understand the words of Solomon: 'Draw me; we will run after you' (Song 1:4). Jesus, there is no need then to say: 'In drawing me, draw all the souls I love.' The words 'Draw me' suffice. I dare therefore to borrow your own words which you used on your last night as a traveller on earth: 'I have manifested your name to the men whom you have given me out of the world. They were yours and you gave them to me; and they have kept your word. Now they know that all which you have given me is from you, because the words you gave me I have given to them and they have received them . . . I pray for them . . . and not for them only do I pray, but for those also who through their word will believe in me . . . I have made known your name to them and will make it known, that the love with which you have loved me may be in them and I in them' (see John 17).

I would repeat your words before losing myself in your love. Perhaps I am very daring, but for a long time you have allowed me to be daring. You have said to me, as the father to the prodigal son: 'All I have is yours' (Luke 15:31). Therefore I may use your own words to draw down favours from your Father in heaven upon all the souls under my care.

Thérèse of Lisieux

More on 'Draw me'

I have not fully explained my thoughts on: 'Draw me, and we will run.' The Lord has said: 'No one comes to me unless the Father who has sent me draws him' (John 6:44), and further on he tells us: 'Everyone who asks shall receive; he that seeks shall find; and the one who knocks shall have it opened to him' (Matthew 7:8). And again he adds: 'If you ask the Father anything in my name, he will give it to you' (John 16:23).

No doubt it was for this reason that, long before the birth of Jesus, the Holy Spirit inspired these prophetic words: 'Draw me – we will run.'

In asking to be drawn, we seek an intimate union with the object that has led our heart captive. If iron and fire were endowed with reason, and the iron could say 'Draw me', would this not prove its wish to be identified with the fire to the point of sharing its substance? Well, such precisely is my prayer.

I ask Jesus to draw me into the fire of his love, and to unite me so closely to himself that he may live and act in me. I feel the more the fire of love consumes my heart, the more frequently I shall cry 'Draw me!' and the more will those souls who come into contact with mine run swiftly.

Thérèse of Lisieux

The test of solid virtue

When you are exposed to all sorts of criticism and unjust accusations, go on in your own way without making any change in your conduct.

This is truly to live by faith alone with God in the midst of the bustle and confusion of creatures.

In such a condition exterior things can never penetrate to the interior, and neither flattery nor contempt can disturb the peace that you enjoy.

This is to live a truly interior life. As long as this state of independence has not been acquired, virtues that have a most attractive appearance are not really solid, but very superficial, and liable to be overthrown by the faintest breath of inconsistency or contradiction.

Be well on your guard against all illusions which aim at making you follow your own ideas and prefer yourself to others. The spirit of self-sufficiency and criticism of one's neighbour seems to many persons a mere trifle; but it is much opposed to religious simplicity, and it hinders many souls from attempting an interior life. It is not possible, in fact, to begin this life without the help of the Holy Spirit, who only communicates himself to the humble, the simple, and those who are little in their own eyes.

Jean-Pierre de Caussade

Raised by God's mercy

Mercy is a work which springs from the goodness of God, and it will continue to work until sin is no longer allowed to molest faithful souls. When sin no longer has licence, then the work of mercy will cease. Then shall every soul be gathered into goodness and rest there for ever.

Under his watchfulness we fall; by his blessed love and strength and wisdom we are defended; and through mercy and through grace we are lifted up to many joys.

Whenever we contemplate what is forbidden, our Lord touches us tenderly and calls us kindly, saying to our soul, 'Forget this fancy. Turn to me. I am enough for you. Rejoice in your Saviour and your salvation.'

This is our Lord's will: that we trust him and search for him, enjoy him and delight in him, and comfort and strengthen ourselves, as by his help and grace we may, until such time as we see him face to face.

Julian of Norwich

Trust

The Lord Jesus Christ
appeared to me in a vision
when I was in distress; he sat
on my bedside wearing a
cloak of purple silk. He
looked at me with so much
love that I felt his strength
flow into my spirit and he
said, 'Why have you forsaken
me, when I have never abandoned you?'

Blessed be Jesus who is always near in times of stress.
Even when we cannot feel his presence he is close.

Jesus said within my heart, 'I will never leave you
either in happiness or distress. I will always be there
to help you and watch over you. Nothing in heaven
or earth can part you from me.'

'When you are quiet and still I can speak to your
heart.'

Margery Kempe

On eating and sleeping

Remember the words of our Lord: 'Eat and drink what they provide' (Luke 10:8). I think there is more profit in eating whatever is offered you, whether it suits your taste or not, than in always choosing the worst. Though the latter practice seems more austere, the former is more submissive, because this kind of mortification makes no display, gives no offence and is especially suitable for one living in society.

It is in this indifference as to what we eat and drink that we shall follow the spirit of that precept: 'Eat and drink what they provide.'

Everyone should take that just proportion of sleep at night which he requires for being usefully awake in the day. Scripture, the example of the saints and our natural reason all commend the morning as the best and most profitable part of the day.

I recommend you to go to rest early at night, so that you may be awake and rise early in the morning, which is the pleasantest and least cumbered time of the day.

Early rising is more profitable both to health and holiness.

Francis de Sales

The gospel – its cost

I have given up everything.

There is only one thing left, my weak and broken body.

If they take that away, they will make me the poorer by an hour of life, perhaps two hours.

Nevertheless, my soul they cannot take.

I know perfectly well that from the beginning of the world the word of Christ has been of such a kind that whoever wants to carry the gospel into the world must necessarily, like the apostles before them, renounce everything, even expect death at any and every hour.

If it were not so, it would not be the word of Christ.

By death the gospel was bought, by deaths spread abroad, by deaths safeguarded.

In like manner it must take many deaths to preserve it, even to restore it.

Christ is a bloody partnership for us.

Martin Luther

The necessity of the Spirit

As all merit is in the Son of God, in what he has done and suffered for us, so all power is in the Spirit of God. And therefore every man, in order to believe unto salvation, must receive the Holy Ghost. This is essentially necessary to every Christian, not in order to his working miracles, but in order to faith, peace, joy and love – the ordinary fruits of the Spirit.

Although no man on earth can explain the particular manner wherein the Spirit of God works on the soul, yet whosoever has these fruits cannot but know and *feel* that God has wrought them in his heart. Sometimes he acts more particularly on the understanding, opening or enlightening it (as the Scripture speaks), and revealing, unveiling, discovering to us 'the deep things of God'.

Sometimes he acts on the wills and affections of men; withdrawing them from evil, inclining them to good, inspiring (breathing, as it were) good thoughts into them. So it has frequently been expressed, by an easy, natural metaphor, strictly analogous to *ruach*, *pneuma*, *spiritus*, and the words used in most modern tongues also, to denote the third person in the ever-blessed Trinity. But however it be expressed, it is certain all true faith, and the whole work of salvation, every good thought, word, and work, is altogether by the operation of the Spirit of God.

John Wesley

The operations of the Spirit

Many years ago, when one was describing the glorious privilege of a believer, I cried out, 'If this be so, I have no faith'. He replied, 'You have faith, but it is weak'. The very same thing I say to you, my dear friend. You have faith, but it is only as a grain of mustard-seed. Hold fast what you have, and ask for what you want.

There is an irreconcilable variability in the operations of the Holy Spirit on the souls of men, more especially as to the manner of justification. Many find him rushing upon them like a torrent, while they experience 'the o'erwhelming power of saving grace'. This has been the experience of many.

But in others he works in a very different way:

'He deigns his influence to infuse,
Sweet, refreshing, as the silent dews.'

It has pleased him to work the latter way in you from the beginning, and it is not improbable he will continue (as he has begun) to work in a gentle and almost insensible manner.

Let him take his own way. He is wiser than you; he will do all things well. Do not reason against him, but let the prayer of your heart be,

'Mould as thou wilt thy passive clay.'

John Wesley

The strength of peace of the soul

The great principle of the interior life is the peace of the soul, and it must be preserved with such care that the moment it is attacked all else must be put aside and every effort made to try and regain this holy peace.

Peace and tranquillity of mind alone give great strength to the soul to enable it to do all that God wishes, while anxiety and uneasiness make the soul feeble and languid, and as though sick.

Then one feels neither taste for, nor attraction to virtue, but, on the contrary, disgust and discouragement of which the devil does not fail to take advantage. For this reason he uses all his cunning to deprive us of peace, and under a thousand specious pretexts, at one time about self-examination, or sorrow for sin, at another about the way we continually neglect grace, or that by our own fault we make no progress; that God will, at last, forsake us.

This is why masters of the spiritual life lay down this great principle to distinguish the true inspirations of God from those that emanate from the devil; that the former are always sweet and peaceful, inducing to confidence and humility, while the latter are intense, restless and violent, leading to discouragement and mistrust, or else to presumption and self-will.

Jean-Pierre de Caussade

Wondering delight in God

I saw, too, that his unceasing work in every thing is done so well, so wisely, and so mightily that it is beyond our power to imagine, guess, or think.

When by his grace our courteous Lord shows himself to our soul, then we have what we desire and for the time we see nothing more to pray for, but all our mind and strength is gathered up in the sight of him. This is a high, unimaginable prayer in my sight.

Truth sees God, wisdom beholds God and from these two comes a third, a holy wondering delight in God, which is love. Where there is truth and wisdom there also is true love, springing from them both.

When we die we shall come to God knowing ourselves clearly, having God wholly. We shall be enfolded in God for ever, seeing him truly, feeling him fully, hearing him spiritually, smelling him delectably, and tasting him sweetly.

Julian of Norwich

The river of time

One can love the world, or love God: if we love the world there is no room in our heart for the love of God; we cannot love God and the world, which passes away with its loves.

You ask, 'Why should I not love the world, since God made it?' Brethren, a man loves God too little who loves anything except for God's sake: it is not that created things may not be loved, but to love them for themselves is cupidity, not love.

Choose: either love the things of time, and pass away with them, or do not love them, and live for ever with God.

The river of time sweeps on, but there, like a tree planted by the water, is our Lord Jesus Christ. He became man, willing to plant himself by the river of time.

If you feel yourself drifting down to the rapids, lay hold of the tree; if you are caught up in the love of the world, hold on to Christ. He for your sake entered into time, but he did not cease to be eternal.

Augustine

Hearing the Spirit

Every time I hear a robin
sing, I am filled with
thankfulness and praise.

One day in church I was
surrounded by such a sweet
atmosphere I felt that if it
continued I could live without
food and drink.

I heard a noise like wind blowing in my ears and
knew it for the sound of the Holy Spirit which
became like the voice of a dove.

When the Lord spoke to me I lost all sense of time.
I did not know if he was with me five or six hours
or only one. It was so holy and full of grace that I
felt as if I had been in heaven.

Margery Kempe

A mistaken atonement theology

They who suppose the wrath and anger of God upon fallen man to be a state of mind in God himself, to be a political kind of just indignation, a point of honourable resentment which the sovereign Deity, as Governor of the world, ought not to recede from but must have a sufficient satisfaction done to his offended authority before he can (consistently with his sovereign honour) receive the sinner into his favour, hold the doctrine of the necessity of Christ's atoning life and death in a mistaken sense.

That many good souls may hold this doctrine in this simplicity of belief I make no manner of doubt. But when books are written to impose and require this belief of others as the only saving faith in the life and death of Christ, it is then an error that ceases to be innocent.

For neither reason nor Scripture will allow us to bring wrath into God himself, as a temper of his mind, who is only infinite, unalterable, overflowing love, as unchangeable in love as he is in power and goodness.

William Law

The fruit of the Spirit

Let none ever presume to rest in any supposed testimony of the Spirit which is separate from the fruit of it. If the Spirit of God does really testify that we are the children of God, the immediate consequence will be the fruit of the Spirit, even 'love, joy, peace, long-suffering, gentleness, goodness, fidelity, meekness, temperance'.

And however this fruit may be clouded for a while during the time of strong temptation, so that it does not appear to the tempted person, while Satan is sifting him as wheat; yet the substantial part of it remains, even under the thickest cloud.

It is true, joy in the Holy Ghost may be withdrawn during the hour of trial; yea, the soul may be 'exceeding sorrowful' while 'the hour and power of darkness' continue; but even this is generally restored with increase, till we rejoice 'with joy unspeakable and full of glory'.

Let none rest in any supposed fruit of the Spirit without the witness. When we have once received this Spirit of adoption, this 'peace which passeth all understanding' will 'keep our hearts and minds in Christ Jesus'. And when this has brought forth its genuine fruit, all inward and outward holiness, it is undoubtedly the will of him that calleth us to give us always what he has once given.

John Wesley

The eleventh showing

And with this same look of joy and happiness, our good Lord looked down to his right and made me remember where our Lady stood at the time of his Passion. And he said: 'Would you like to see her?'

And in these sweet words it was as if he said: 'I know full well that you would like to see my blessed mother, for she is the greatest delight, after myself, that I could show you – the one dearest to me and the one who gives me highest praise. She is most worth seeing of all that I have made.'

And because of the high and wonderful love he had specially for this sweet maiden, his blessed mother, our Lady Saint Mary, he showed her greatly rejoicing, as if he used words that said: 'Would you like to see how I love her, so that you can rejoice with me in the love I have for her, and she for me?'

And, so that we should understand even better, our Lord speaks to all mankind who shall be saved as if they were all just one person – as though he said: 'Can you see in her how you yourself are loved? It was for love of you that I made her so high, so noble and so good. And this brings me great joy, and I want it to bring you joy, too.'

Julian of Norwich

God, the boundless abyss of all that is good

God, considered in himself, is as infinitely separate from all possibility of doing hurt or willing pain to any creature as he is from a possibility of suffering pain or hurt from the hand of man.

This is because he is in himself, in his holy Trinity, nothing else but the boundless abyss of all that is good and sweet and amiable, and therefore stands in the utmost contrariety to everything that is not a blessing – in an eternal impossibility of willing and intending a moment's pain or hurt to any creature.

For from this unbounded source of goodness and perfection nothing but infinite streams of blessing are perpetually flowing forth upon all nature and creatures in a more incessant plenty than rays of light stream from the sun.

And as the sun has but one nature and can give forth nothing but the blessings of light, so the holy triune God has but one nature and intent towards all the creation, which is to pour forth the riches and sweetness of his divine perfections upon everything that is capable of them and according to its capacity to receive them.

William Law

God, the fountain of all good

God is the Good, the unchangeable, overflowing fountain of Good that sends forth nothing but Good to all eternity. He is the love itself, the unmixed, unmeasurable love, doing nothing but from love, giving nothing but gifts of love to everything that he has made; requiring nothing of all his creatures but the spirit and fruits of that love which brought them into being.

Oh, how sweet is this contemplation of the height and depth of the riches of divine love! With what attraction must it draw every thoughtful man to return love for love to this overflowing fountain of boundless goodness!

View every part of our redemption, from Adam's first sin to the resurrection of the dead, and you will find nothing but successive mysteries of that first love which created angels and men. All the mysteries of the gospel are only so many marks and proofs of God's desiring to make his love triumph in the removal of sin and disorder from all nature and creatures.

William Law

That feeling of security!

A very treacherous temptation is a feeling of security that we shall never relapse into our former faults or care for worldly pleasures again. We say to ourselves: 'Now I know what the world is, that all it contains passes away, and I care more for divine things.'

This temptation is the most dangerous of all, especially at the beginning of the religious life. Such souls, feeling safe, do not avoid customary occasions of sin which they enter blindfold, and God grant they may not fall lower than ever before, and that they may rise again. This the demon, seeing the harm they may do him and the good they may do their neighbour, will use every means in his power to prevent.

What, O eternal Father! can we do, except have recourse to thee and beg thee not to permit our enemies to lead us into temptation? You will be freed more quickly from temptation if you are near our Lord than if you were far off. Beg and entreat this freedom of him, as you do every day in the Paternoster.

Teresa of Avila

Strength and safety lie in the love and fear of God

Give us, kind Master, some safeguard that we may live without overwhelming terror amid such perilous warfare.

The safeguards we may use, daughters, given us by His Majesty, are love and fear.

Love will make us quicken our steps and fear will lead us to look where we set our feet down lest we trip against the many stumbling-blocks on the road by which all who live must travel. Thus armed, we shall be safe against deception.

The soul that truly loves God loves all good, seeks all good, protects all good, praises all good, joins itself to good men, helps and defends them, and embraces all the virtues: it only loves what is true and worth loving.

Do you think it possible that one who truly loves God cares, or can care, for vanities, or riches, or worldly things, or pleasures or honours? Neither can such a soul quarrel or feel envy, for it aims at nothing save pleasing its Beloved.

It dies with longing for his love and gives its life in striving how to please him better.

Teresa of Avila

Spiritual respiration

God is continually breathing, as it were, upon the soul; and his soul is breathing unto God. Grace is descending into his heart, and prayer and praise ascending to heaven: and by this intercourse between God and man, this fellowship with the Father and the Son, as by a kind of spiritual respiration, the life of God in the soul is sustained; and the child of God grows up, till he comes to the 'full measure of the stature of Christ'.

From hence it manifestly appears what is the nature of the new birth. It is that great change which God works in the soul when he brings it into life, when he raises it from the death of sin to the life of righteousness.

It is the change wrought in the whole soul by the almighty Spirit of God when it is 'created anew in Christ Jesus'; when it is 'renewed after the image of God in righteousness and true holiness'; when the love of the world is changed into the love of God; pride into humility; passion into meekness; hatred, envy, malice, into a sincere, tender, disinterested love for all mankind.

In a word, it is that change whereby the earthly, sensual, devilish mind is turned into the 'mind which was in Christ Jesus'. This is the nature of the new birth: 'So is every one that is born of the Spirit.'

John Wesley

Giving

If you give something to someone who is in need then let a cheerful face precede your gift, along with kind words and encouragement for his suffering.

When you do this, the pleasure he feels in his mind at your gift will be greater than the needs of his body.

A person who, while having God in mind, honours everyone, will find everyone to be his helper, thanks to the hidden will of God.

Someone who speaks in defence of a person who suffers injustice will find an advocate in his Creator.

Whoever gives a hand to help his neighbour is helped by God's own hand.

But the person who accuses his brother for his evil deeds will find God as his accuser.

Isaac of Syria

A sharp dart of longing love

Of God himself no man can think. He may well be loved, but not thought.

By love he may be grasped and held; by thought never.

Although it is good at times to think specially of the kindness and goodness of God, and although this may enlighten you and play a part in contemplation, nevertheless in this work such thoughts shall be put down and covered with a cloud of forgetting.

You are to step above them boldly and eagerly, and with a devout and lively impulse of love you are to try to pierce the darkness above you.

Smite upon that thick cloud of unknowing with a sharp dart of longing love.

Come what may, do not give up.

Author of 'The Cloud of Unknowing'

Him I covet, him I seek, and him alone

If any thought should arise and continually press above you and between you and the darkness, and if it should say to you: 'What are you looking for? What would you have?', then make answer that it is God whom you would have.

'Him I covet, him I seek, and him alone.'

And if the thought should ask you, 'What is that God?', then you are to say that it is the God who made you, and bought you, and who has graciously called you to his love.

'And in him', you may say to this thought, 'you have no power over me.'

Therefore say to him, 'Get down again,' and tread him down quickly with a stirring of love.

You are to do this even though he seems to you to be a truly holy thought, and even though it seems that he would help you to seek God.

Author of 'The Cloud of Unknowing'

St Columba at Iona

Delightful I think it to be in the bosom of an isle
on the crest of a rock,
that I may see often
the calm of the sea.

That I may see its heavy waves
over the glittering ocean
as they chant a melody to their Father
on their eternal course.

That I may see its ebb and its flood-tide
in its flow;
that this should be my name, a secret I declare,
'He who turned his back on Ireland.'

That I may bless the Lord
who has power over all,
heaven with its crystal orders of angels,
earth, ebb, flood-tide.

That I may pore on one of my books,
good for my soul,
a while kneeling for beloved heaven,
a while at psalms.

A while meditating upon the Prince of Heaven.

The Celtic Tradition

The unprofitable servant

I call upon you, O God, my mercy, you who created me, and did not forget me when I forgot you. Let me know you, for you are the God who knows me; you are the power of my soul, come into it and make it fit for yourself. This is my hope.

I beg you to come into my heart, for by inspiring it to long for you, you make it ready to receive you.

Now as I call upon you, do not desert me, for you came to my aid before I called for you. When I was far from you, you persuaded me to listen to your voice, to turn back to you.

I called upon you for help, but all the time it was you who were calling me to yourself. You blotted out all my sins and did not repay me with the punishments I deserved.

I was nothing, you need not have given me being; before I was you were, you had no need of me. My service has not the value of a countryman's who tills his master's land, for if I do not serve you with my labour, your work still bears fruit.

I can only serve you and worship you with the good that comes from you. It is from you alone that I receive it, for but for you I should have no being.

Augustine

God looks upon the love
behind the work

[Brother Lawrence said]:

That we ought, once and for all, heartily to put our whole trust in God, and make a full surrender of ourselves to him, secure that he would not deceive us.

We ought not to be weary of doing little things for the love of God, who regards not the greatness of the work, but the love with which it is performed.

We should not wonder if, in the beginning, we often failed in our endeavours, but that at last we should gain a habit, which will naturally produce its acts in us, without our care, and to our exceeding great delight.

The whole substance of religion was faith, hope and love, by the practice of which we become united to the will of God.

All besides is indifferent, and to be used only as a means that we may arrive at our end, and be swallowed up therein by faith and love.

Brother Lawrence

On society and solitude

To seek the society of others or to shun it are both extremes for those who live in the world, and I speak to them now. If we shun others, we indicate disdain and contempt for them. If we seek others, we are in danger of idleness and inactivity. As a sign that we love ourselves we should be content with our own society, content to be alone.

If you are not called to go out to meet people, remain by yourself and contemplate. But if you are asked to meet others, go in God's sight and mix with a free and loving heart.

The kind of people we meet will vary. Some groups are simply formed for recreation; we can join with them, but not to excess. Some we meet for courtesy's sake, getting to know our neighbours, being about unostentatiously, but fulfilling our friendly duty. Some are groups of believers and pious people. If we associate with holy people we imbibe their good qualities. It is a great advantage to associate with the truly devout.

You may retire into solitude within yourself, even when you are in company. But in addition, you should seek the solitude of your room, your garden or anywhere else you can find.

Francis de Sales

The living flame

O living flame of love
That wounds so tenderly
In my soul's deepest centre.
As you are no longer oppressive
Perfect your work in me if it is your will.
Break the web of this sweet encounter.

Before the divine fire enters the soul and becomes
one with its depths, the Holy Spirit wounds it,
destroying and consuming the imperfections of its
evil habits.

The soul suffers greatly in this, for in this state of
purification the flame does not burn brightly but in
darkness, and if it gives any light at all it is only
to show up and make the soul experience its own
weaknesses and defects.

It is not a refreshing, peaceful fire, but a consuming
and searching one that makes the soul grieve at the
sight of itself. The soul perceives its own smallness
in comparison with the immensity of the flame.

John of the Cross

God is our deepest centre

The centre of the soul is God. When the soul loves and understands and enjoys God to its utmost capacity it will have reached its deep centre, God.

Love unites the soul with God; and the more love the soul has, the more powerfully it enters into God and is centred on him.

The soul which has one degree of love is clearly in its centre, God, since one degree is sufficient for it to abide in him through grace. If it has two degrees it enters into another more interior centre with God, and so on. If it reaches the last degree, the love of God will be able to wound the soul at its deepest point; that is, it is brought to the state where it appears to be God himself.

In this state the soul is like a crystal, limpid and pure. It is so enlightened it appears to be light itself.

John of the Cross

The thirteenth showing

After this, the Lord brought into my mind the longing I had for him before, and I saw that nothing stood in my way but sin, and I saw this was the same for all of us. And it seemed to me that, if sin had not been, we should all have been clean and like our Lord, the way he made us. And so, in my folly, before this time I had often wondered why, by the great foreseeing wisdom of God, the beginning of sin was not prevented, for then, I thought, all should have been well.

I should have left off this worrying; nevertheless, I mourned and sorrowed over it without reason or discretion. But Jesus, who in the showing told me all that I needed, answered by this word and said: 'Sin is behovely – it had to be – but all shall be well, and all shall be well, and all manner of thing shall be well.'

In this stark word 'sin' our Lord brought to my mind all things in general that are not good – and the shame, the despising and the utter stripping he accepted for us in this life, and his dying. He also brought to mind all the bodily and spiritual pains and passions of all his creatures.

For we are all stripped in part and shall be, while we follow our master Jesus until we are made pure. That is to say, until we are stripped of our mortal flesh, and of all our inner desires that are not wholly good.

Julian of Norwich

The cause of pain is sin

And all this was shown in a moment and was quickly turned into comfort, for our Lord God does not want the soul to be frightened by this ugly sight. But I did not see sin. For I believe it has no kind of substance or manner of being and that it is only known through the pain it causes. And as for pain, as I see it, it is something temporary, for it cleanses us and makes us know ourselves and ask for forgiveness. And throughout all this the Passion of our Lord comforts us, and it is his blessed will it should do so.

And because of our good Lord's tender love to all those who shall be saved, he quickly comforts them, saying: 'The cause of all this pain is sin. But all shall be well, and all shall be well, and all manner of thing shall be well.' These words were said so kindly and without a hint of blame to me or to any who shall be saved. So how unjust would it be for me to blame God for allowing me to sin, when he does not blame me for falling into it.

And in these words I saw a wonderful high secret hidden in God, and that he will show us this secret openly in heaven. When we know this secret we shall truly see the reason he allowed sin to be, and in the knowledge of this we shall rejoice endlessly in our Lord God.

Julian of Norwich

Cleansing through suffering

So I saw that Christ has compassion on us because of sin. And just as, before this, I was filled with pain and compassion during Christ's Passion, in the same way I was filled full of compassion for all my fellow-Christians – for those much, much-loved people who shall be saved, that is to say. For God's servants, Holy Church, shall be shaken in sorrow and anguish and tribulation in this world, as a cloth is shaken in the wind. And as to this, our Lord answered in this way: 'I shall make a great occasion out of this in heaven, of endless honour and everlasting joy.'

Yes, I saw so much, that I understood that our Lord, in his pity and compassion, can be pleased by his servants' tribulation. He lays upon every one he longs to bring into his bliss something that is no blame in his sight, but for which they are blamed and despised in this world – scorned, mocked and cast out. He does this to offset the harm they should otherwise have from the pomp and vainglory of this earthly life, and to make their road to him easier, and to bring them higher in his joy without end.

For he says, 'I shall shatter all your vain affections and your vicious pride, and after that I shall gather you up and make you kind and gentle, clean and holy, by joining you to me.'

Julian of Norwich

Conversion

June 18th, 1735, being in secret prayer, I felt suddenly my heart melting within me like wax before the fire with love to God my Saviour; and also felt not only love, peace, etc., but longing to be dissolved, and to be with Christ; then was a cry in my inmost soul, which I was totally unacquainted with before, Abba Father! Abba Father! I could not help calling God my Father; I knew that I was his child, and that He loved me, and heard me. My soul being filled and satiated, crying, ' 'Tis enough, I am satisfied. Give me strength, and I will follow thee through fire and water.' I could say I was happy indeed! There was in me a well of water, springing up to everlasting life (John 4:14). The love of God was shed abroad in my heart by the Holy Ghost (Romans 5:5).

The Celtic Tradition

Sayings

The prayer of someone who harbours a grudge is a seed upon a stone.

An ascetic without compassion is a tree that bears no fruit.

A rebuke springing from envy is a poisoned arrow.

The praise of a crafty man is a hidden snare.

A foolish counsellor is a blind watchman: a wise counsellor is a wall of confidence.

Live with vultures rather than with the covetous: live amidst lions rather than among the proud.

Be persecuted, rather than be a persecutor.
Be crucified, rather than be a crucifier.
Be treated unjustly, rather than treat anyone unjustly.
Be oppressed, rather than be an oppressor.
Be gentle, rather than zealous.
Lay hold of goodness, rather than justice.

Isaac of Syria

The inward new man

All our salvation consists in the manifestation of the nature, life and spirit of Jesus Christ in our inward new man. This alone is Christian redemption, this alone redeems, renews and regains the first life of God in the soul of man. Everything besides this is self, is fiction, is propriety, is own will, and however coloured is only your old man, with all his deeds.

Enter therefore with all your heart into this truth, let your eye be always upon it, do everything in view of it, try everything by the truth of it, love nothing but for the sake of it. Wherever you go, whatever you do, at home or abroad, in the field or at church, do all in a desire of union with Christ, in imitation of his tempers and inclinations, and look upon all as nothing but that which exercises and increases the spirit and life of Christ in your soul.

William Law

The Law and the gospel differentiated

In this verse (Psalm 85:5) the difference between Law and gospel is foreshadowed.

The Law is the word of Moses *to* us, the gospel is the word of God *within* us.

The former abides outside us: it addresses us in figures of speech, in forecasts of things to come.

The latter takes up its abode within us, and speaks of inward and spiritual things, and truth.

The one is speaking *within* us, the other speaks *to* us.

The righteousness of the Law is earthly, it is concerned with earthly affairs, and consists of our doing good works . . . The heavenly passive righteousness does not spring from our own efforts. We receive it from heaven. We do not produce it: we receive it in faith.

The Law is the ministry of the letter, the gospel the ministry of the Spirit: the letter killeth, but the Spirit giveth life.

Martin Luther

Hermit prayer

O Son of the living God, old eternal King, I desire a hidden hut in the wilderness that it may be my home.

A narrow little blue stream beside it and a clear pool for the washing away of sin through the grace of the Holy Ghost.

A lovely wood close about it on every side, to nurse birds with all sorts of voices and to hide them with its shelter.

Looking south for heat, and a stream through its land, and good fertile soil suitable for all plants.

A beautiful draped church, a home for God from Heaven, and bright lights above the clean white Gospels.

Enough of clothing and food from the King of fair fame, and to be sitting for a while and praying to God in every place.

The Celtic Tradition

The lever of prayer

We shall run together because souls that are on fire can never remain inactive. They may, like Mary Magdalene, sit at the feet of Jesus, listening to his words. Though appearing to give him nothing, they give him far more than Martha, who was 'troubled about many things' (Luke 10:41).

It is not, of course, Martha's work that the Lord blames, for his own Mother humbly devoted herself to the self-same duty, having to prepare the meals for the Holy Family. What he does blame is Martha's excessive solicitude.

The power of prayer has been understood by all the saints. Was it not in prayer that St Paul, St Augustine, St Thomas Aquinas, St John of the Cross, St Teresa and so many other friends of God acquired the wonderful knowledge which has enthralled the loftiest minds?

'Give me a lever and a fulcrum on which to rest it,' said Archimedes, 'and I will lift the world.' What the scientist could not obtain, because his request had a merely material end without reference to God, the saints have obtained in all its fullness. God has given them a fulcrum to lean upon himself alone, and for a lever the prayer which inflames with the fire of love. Thus they have uplifted the world, and on earth will continue to raise it till the end of time.

Thérèse of Lisieux

Grace

Jesus said to me, 'My grace in you is like the sun. Sometimes the sun shines brightly so that everyone can see it, at other times it is hidden behind a cloud; although you cannot see it, the brightness is still there. In the same way my grace is always with you.'

'My grace is always with you. Anyone who does the will of God, is my brother and sister and mother (Mark 3:35). When you try to please me, then you are a daughter. When you feel the pain of my Passion, then you are a mother having compassion on her child. When you weep for other people's troubles you are a sister and when you long to be with me in heaven, then you are a wife who has no happiness apart from her husband.'

'If you trust me you will receive my grace in abundance.'

Margery Kempe

Liking and loving others

I have noticed that it is the holiest who are most loved: everyone seeks their company and is on the watch to do them a service without waiting to be asked. Holy people who can bear to be treated with a want of respect and attention find themselves surrounded by an atmosphere of love. St John of the Cross says: 'All good things have come to me since I no longer seek them for myself.'

Imperfect people, on the other hand, are left alone. They receive the measure of politeness, but their company is avoided for fear a word spoken will hurt their feelings. When I say imperfect people, I mean those who, being supersensitive or wanting in tact or refinement, make life unpleasant for others. Defects of this kind seem incurable.

From this I conclude that I ought to seek the companionship of those for whom I have a natural aversion. Frequently it needs only a word or a smile to impart fresh life in a despondent soul. But it is not just to bring consolation that I try to be kind. I wish to please the Lord's gospel precept: 'When you make a feast, call the poor, the maimed, the blind and the lame, and you will be blessed, because they have nothing with which to recompense you, and your Father who sees in secret will repay you' (see Luke 14:13–14).

Thérèse of Lisieux

The way God works

A Dominican anchorite at Lynn said:

'Do not be afraid of anything, our Lord will take care of you himself. Even when all your friends have deserted you he will be there.'

'For the good of your soul God has made some people to be a scourge to you. Just as a blacksmith can file rusty iron until it shines clean and bright, so the more these people try you, the brighter you will shine before God.'

'God has chosen me to look after you; be humble and courteous and thank God at all times.'

'Even if God takes away all your tears and withdraws your conversations from you, yet still you must believe that God loves you and because of the favours he has already shown you, you can be certain that you will be with him in heaven.'

Margery Kempe

Beware of flattery

Unless you are careful, praise from others may harm you greatly, for when once it begins it never ceases, and generally ends in running you down afterwards. This usually takes the form of telling you that you are more holy than others and suchlike flattering speeches.

For the love of God, I implore you never to find your peace in such speeches for you might come to believe them, or to think you had done all you need and that your work was finished.

Remember how the world treated our Lord Jesus Christ, yet how it had extolled him on Palm Sunday! Men so esteemed St John the Baptist as to mistake him for the Messiah, yet how barbarously and for what a motive they afterwards beheaded him!

Always struggle within your own heart against these dangerous flatteries, then you will go forth with deeper humility.

May God, of his great bounty, give us light.

Teresa of Avila

On hasty judgement

'Judge not, that you may not be judged' were our Saviour's words. Rash judgements are most displeasing to God. Men's judgements are rash, because we are not one another's judges but usurp our Lord's right.

But it is necessary to judge ourselves. St Paul says, 'If we judged ourselves truly, we should not be judged' (1 Corinthians 11:31).

We must ask why we make rash judgements. Some of us are naturally bitter and harsh, and we could do with sound spiritual advice, because this imperfection is hard to overcome.

Some judge harshly out of pride, putting themselves up by putting others down. Some view the faults of others with complacency in order to enhance their own virtues. Others judge by feeling, thinking well of those they like, and ill of those they dislike. Jealousy, fear, ambition and other weaknesses tend to excite rash judgement.

The remedy is charity. Rash judgement is a spiritual jaundice which makes things appear evil. The cure is to apply love. If your heart is gentle, your judgement will be gentle; if it is loving, so will your judgement be.

Francis de Sales

Praise

Almighty Creator, who hast
  made all things,
The world cannot express all
  thy glories,
Even though the grass and
  the trees should sing.

The Father has wrought so
  great a multitude of
  wonders
That they cannot be equalled.
No letters can contain them, no letters can express
  them.

He who made the wonder of the world
Will save us, has saved us.
It is not too great toil to praise the Trinity.

Purely, humbly, in skilful verse
I should delight to give praise to the Trinity.

It is not too great toil to praise the Son of Mary.

The Celtic Tradition

The work of patience

What may we understand by the work of patience? 'Let patience have its perfect work.' It seems to mean, let it have its full fruit or effect. And what is the fruit which the Spirit of God is accustomed to produce hereby, in the heart of a believer? One immediate fruit of patience is peace: a sweet tranquillity of mind, a serenity of spirit, which can never be found unless where patience reigns.

And this peace often rises into joy. Even in the midst of various temptations, those that are enabled 'in patience to possess their souls' can witness not only quietness of spirit, but triumph and exultation.

Christian zeal is likewise confirmed and increased by patience, and so is activity in every good work, the same Spirit inciting us to be 'patient in bearing ill, and doing well'; making us equally willing to do and suffer the whole will of God.

But what is the *perfect* work of patience? Is it anything less than 'the perfect love of God' constraining us to love every soul of man, 'even as Christ loved us'?

John Wesley

True resignation

We ought quietly to suffer whatever befalls us, to bear the defects of others and our own, to confess them to God in secret prayer, or with groans which cannot be uttered; but never to speak a sharp or peevish word, nor to murmur or repine.

We are to bear with those we cannot amend and to be content with offering them to God. This is true resignation. And since he has borne our infirmities we may well bear those of each other for his sake.

To abandon all, to strip one's self of all, in order to seek and to follow Jesus Christ naked to Bethlehem, where he was born: naked to the hall where he was scourged: and naked to Calvary where he died on the cross, is so great a mercy that neither the thing nor the knowledge of it is given to any but through faith in the Son of God.

John Wesley

A true and false desire

Do not all Christians desire to have Christ to be their Saviour? Yes. But here is the deceit; all would have Christ to be their Saviour in the *next* world and to help them into heaven when they die by his power and merits with God.

But this is not willing Christ to be your Saviour; for his salvation, if it is to be had, must be had in *this* world; if he saves you it must be done in this life by changing all that is within you, by helping you to a new heart, as he helped the blind to see, the lame to walk and the dumb to speak.

For to have salvation from Christ is nothing else but to be made like unto him; it is to have his humility and meekness, his mortification and self-denial, his renunciation of the spirit, wisdom and honours of this world, his love of God, his desire of doing God's will and seeking only his honour.

To have these tempers formed and begotten in your heart is to have salvation from Christ. But if you will not to have these tempers brought forth in you, if your faith and desire does not seek and cry to Christ for them in the same reality as the lame asked to walk and the blind to see, then you must be said to be unwilling to have Christ to be your Saviour.

William Law

Of true friendship

I bid you love everyone with the love of charity, but have no friendship except with those who can share virtuous love with you. What a good thing it is to love on earth as we shall love in heaven, and learn to cherish one another here as we shall do for ever there.

I am not now talking of the mere love which extends to everyone, but of the spiritual friendship by which two or more share in each other's devotion and spiritual affections, making them of one mind. Such may well say, 'Behold how good and joyful a thing it is to live together in unity.'

Do not *form* any other friendships. I say *form* because you must not forsake or despise those friendships to which you are called by duty among relatives, those connected with you, benefactors and neighbours. I am only speaking of those you select yourself.

Some say it is better to have no special friendships or attachments, that they engross the heart, distract the mind and foster jealousies. But they are mistaken. They have read that individual and excessive friendships are hurtful in religious life, and imagine it to be the same for the rest of the world, but it is not so. In the world it is necessary to be bound together in friendship, to stimulate each other in doing good.

Francis de Sales

Come, drink of the fountain

We must begin prayer by feeling no doubt that unless we allow ourselves to be defeated we are sure to succeed. This is certain, for however insignificant our conquest may be, we shall come off with great gains.

Never fear that the Lord who invites us to drink of the fountain will allow us to die of thirst.

I have said it before and I shall often repeat it, for people who have not learnt our Lord's goodness by experience, but only know of it by faith, are often discouraged.

It is a great grace to have proved for oneself the friendship and caresses he bestows on those who walk by this way of prayer, and how, as it were, he defrays all the costs.

It does not surprise me that those who have never practised it should want the security of receiving some interest. You know that we receive a hundredfold even in this life, and that our Lord said: 'Ask and you shall receive.' If you do not believe him it would be of little use for me to wear myself out with telling you.

Teresa of Avila

How the ground is prepared for this fount of water

If the ground is well dug by troubles, persecutions, detractions and infirmities – they are few who ascend so high without this – if it be well broken up by great detachment from all self-interest, it will drink in so much water that it can hardly ever be parched again.

But if it be ground which is mere waste, and covered with thorns (as I was when I began); if the occasions of sin be not avoided; if it be an ungrateful soil, unfitted for so great a grace, it will be parched up again.

If the gardener becomes careless, and if our Lord, out of his mere goodness, will not send down rain upon it, the garden is ruined.

Thus has it been with me more than once, so that I am amazed at it. I write this for the comfort of souls which are weak, as I am, that they may never despair, nor cease to trust in the power of God; they must not be discouraged, unless they would lose themselves utterly. Tears gain everything, and one drop of water attracts another.

Teresa of Avila

Stability

A brother asked an old man, 'What shall I do, father, for I am not acting like a monk at all, but I eat, drink and sleep, carelessly, and I have evil thoughts and I am in great trouble, passing from one work to another and from one work to another.' The old man said, 'Sit in your cell and do the little you can, untroubled. For I think the little you can do now is of equal value to the great deeds which abba Antony accomplished on the mountain and I believe that by remaining in your cell for the name of God and guarding your conscience, you also will find the place where abba Antony is.'

Sarapion the Sindonite travelled once on a pilgrimage to Rome. Here he was told of a celebrated recluse, a woman who lived always in one small room, never going out. Sceptical about her way of life – for he was himself a great wanderer – Sarapion called on her and asked, 'Why are you sitting here?' To which she replied, 'I am not sitting; I am on a journey.'

The Desert Fathers

The praying believer

He 'prays without ceasing'. It is given him 'always
to pray, and not to faint'. Not that he is always in
the house of prayer, though he neglects no opportunity of being there. Neither is he always on his
knees, although he often is, or on his face, before the
Lord his God. Nor yet is he always crying aloud to
God, or calling upon him in words. For many times
'the Spirit maketh intercession for him with groans
that cannot be uttered'.

But at all times the language of his heart is this:
'Thou brightness of the eternal glory, unto thee is
my heart, though without a voice, and my silence
speaketh unto thee.' And this is true prayer, and this
alone. But his heart is ever lifted up to God, at all
times and in all places.

In this he is never hindered, much less interrupted,
by any person or thing. In retirement or company,
in leisure, business, or conversation, his heart is ever
with the Lord. Whether he lie down or rise up, God
is in all his thoughts. He walks with God continually,
having the loving eye of his mind still fixed upon
him, and everywhere 'seeing him that is invisible'.

John Wesley

Continual prayer

God's command to 'pray without ceasing' is founded on the necessity we have of his grace to preserve the life of God in the soul, which can no more subsist one moment without it than the body can without air.

Whether we think of or speak to God, whether we act or suffer for him, all is prayer when we have no other object than his love and the desire of pleasing him.

All that a Christian does, even in eating and sleeping, is prayer when it is done in simplicity according to the order of God, without either adding to or diminishing it by his own choice.

Prayer continues in the desire of the heart though the understanding be employed on outward things. In souls filled with love the desire to please God is a continual prayer.

John Wesley

Prayer as communion with God

A higher degree of that peace which may well be said to pass all understanding will keep, not only your heart, but all the workings of your mind (as the word properly signifies), both of your reason and imagination, from all irregular sallies. This peace will increase as your faith increases: one always keeps pace with the other. So that on this account also your continual prayer should be, 'Lord, increase my faith!'

A continual desire is a continual prayer – that is, in a low sense of the word; for there is a far higher sense, such an open intercourse with God, such close, uninterrupted communion with him, as Gregory Lopez* experienced, and not a few of our brethren and sisters now alive. One of them (a daughter of sorrow for a long time) was talking with me this morning. This you also should aspire after; as you know, he with whom we have to do is no respecter of persons.

John Wesley

* Gregory Lopez (1611–87) was a Dominican who became the first native Chinese bishop.

Ask, seek, knock

O how meek and gentle, how lowly in heart, how full of love both to God and man, might you have been at this day, if you had only asked – if you had continued instant in prayer! Therefore now, at least, 'ask, and it shall be given unto you'.

Ask that you may thoroughly experience and perfectly practise the whole of that religion which our Lord has here so beautifully described. It shall then be given you to be holy as he is holy, both in heart and in all manner of conversation.

Seek, in the way he hath ordained, in searching the Scriptures, in hearing his word, in meditating thereon, in fasting, in partaking of the Supper of the Lord, and surely you shall find. You shall find that pearl of great price, that faith which overcometh the world, that peace which the world cannot give, that love which is the earnest of your inheritance.

Knock: continue in prayer, and in every other way of the Lord. Be not weary or faint in your mind. Press on to the mark. Take no denial. Let him not go, until he bless you. 'And the door' of mercy, of holiness, of heaven 'shall be opened unto you.'

John Wesley

A short word to be kept intact

If it suits you, you can have this naked intent wrapped up and enfolded in one word. In that case, in order that you may have a better grasp on it, take a short word of one syllable. One syllable is better than two, and the shorter the word the more suited it is to accomplish the work of the spirit.

Such a word is the word 'God' or the word 'Love'. Choose whichever you wish, or another if you prefer, but let it be of one syllable.

Fasten this word to your heart so that it never leaves you, come what may. This word is to be your shield and your spear, whether in peace or in war.

With this word you are to beat upon the cloud and the darkness above you. With it you are to smite down every manner of thought under the cloud of forgetting. So much so, that if any thought should press upon you to ask you what you would have, answer it with no other words but this one word.

And if you should be tempted to analyse this word, answer that you will have it whole and undeveloped. If you will but hold fast, be sure that the temptation will not last long.

Author of 'The Cloud of Unknowing'

God to be loved for himself

It is more profitable for the health of your soul, more worthy in itself, and more pleasing to God and the saints and angels in heaven, and more helpful too to all your friends, bodily or spiritual, living or dead, to experience a blind stirring of love towards God for his own sake, and a secret pressing upon this cloud of unknowing – known and felt in spiritual desire – than to have your inward eye opened in contemplating or beholding all the angels or saints in heaven, or in hearing all the merriment and melody which accompanies their bliss.

But be assured that no man shall have that clear sight in this life; though through the grace of God you may experience feelings in your affection, that is when God chooses to give them. So lift up your love to that cloud, or as I would prefer to say, let God draw your love to it, and endeavour through God's grace to forget everything else.

Author of 'The Cloud of Unknowing'

Sin destroyed at its roots

If, then, you would stand and not fall, never set your intention aside, but strike always with a sharp dart of longing love upon this cloud of unknowing which is between you and your God; and hate to think of anything less than God, and do not leave your work for any reason whatever.

Of all works, it alone – and of itself – destroys sin at its roots.

No matter how much you fast, how long you watch, how early you rise, how hard your bed, how rough your clothes – all this will not help you a whit. The impulse and stirring of sin will still be in you.

And yet more. No matter how much you weep in sorrow for your sins, or for the Passion of Christ, and no matter how much you are mindful of the joys of heaven, although you would find here much good, help, profit and grace, yet in comparison with this blind stirring of love – or without it – it can do but little.

Author of 'The Cloud of Unknowing'

Purification of motive

This blind impulse of love not only destroys the root and ground of sin so far as is possible in this life, but it also begets the virtues.

All virtue is thereby delicately infused, and is known and experienced without any corruption of motive.

No matter how many virtues a man may have, they will be imperfect and in some degree tainted unless they are rooted in this work.

Virtue is nothing else but an ordered and measured affection directed towards God for his sake alone.

He himself is the foundation of all virtues; so much so that if any man be stirred to any one virtue by a mixture of motives – even though God himself be the chief – then that virtue is imperfect.

The two virtues, humility and charity, are good examples and may stand for the others. Whoever has these clearly needs no more. For he has them all.

Author of 'The Cloud of Unknowing'

Tested by falling

And then he allows some of us to fall more severely and distressingly than before – at least that is how we see it. And then it seems to us, who are not always wise, that all we set our hands to is lost. But it is not so. We need to fall, and we need to see that  we have done so. For if we never fell we should not know how weak and pitiable we are in ourselves. Nor should we fully know the wonderful love of our Maker.

In heaven we shall see truly and everlastingly that we have grievously sinned in this life; notwithstanding, we shall see that this in no way diminished his love, nor made us less precious in his sight.

The testing experience of falling will lead us to a deep and wonderful knowledge of the constancy of God's love, which neither can nor will be broken because of sin. To understand this is of great profit.

Julian of Norwich

The danger of self-deception

But then, because of all this spiritual comfort that has been promised, a man or a woman might be led, through folly, to say or think: 'If this is true, then it is good to sin so as to get a better reward', or else to think sin less sinful. Beware of this thinking, for truly if this thought comes it is untrue, and comes from the enemy of that true love that shows us all this comfort.

This same blessed love teaches us that we should hate sin simply for the sake of love. And I am sure, by what I feel myself, that the more every loving soul sees of this, in the courteous love of our Lord God, the less he wants to sin and the more he is ashamed.

For if we had to choose between sin and all the pains of hell, and of purgatory, and of earth – death and the rest – when they were not before us, we should choose to bear all those pains rather than sin. For sin is so vile and so greatly to be hated that it can be likened to no other pain – except the pain that is sin.

And I was shown no harder hell than sin, for there is no hell but sin for a loving soul.

Julian of Norwich

The debtor

We must flee to God in our many tribulations, whatever they may be – domestic worries, ill health,
dangers to those dear to us. The Christian can have
no other refuge but his Saviour, his God. He will
have no strength in himself, but in him in whom he
has taken refuge.

Yet, beloved, among all human tribulations none is
greater than to be conscious of one's sins. If one's
conscience is at peace, one can turn into one's heart
and there find God. But if because of the multitude
of his sins his heart has no rest and God is not there,
where can a man fly in tribulation? If he flies from
the country to the town, from the market place to
his home, anguish follows him.

Wherever he goes he finds his enemy – wherever he
goes he drags himself with him – no troubles are
more bitter than those of conscience.

But even there, God comes to our aid by pardoning
our sins, and our healing lies only in his forgiveness.
If a man owes a great sum of money, he is very
much afraid of what will befall him – his only hope
lies in being forgiven the debt. How much greater
the fear of knowing that we shall perish in paying
the debt of our sins. Beloved, we may be sure of his
forgiveness, only let us not incur that debt again.

Augustine

199

The jumping-off place

The Lord himself has told us in what the perfection of charity consists: 'Greater love has no man, than to give his life for his friends.' But how can one attain to that level of love?

Well, now we know where its perfection lies, let us see where it begins. St John says if a man is rich, and sees his brother in need and hardens his heart, the love of God is not in him. That is where charity begins. If you can't as yet lay down your life for your brother, at least give him some of your goods – not to show off, but from overflowing mercy.

He, your brother, was redeemed as you were by the blood of Christ: he is hungry, in need, perhaps pressed by a creditor, and you have plenty of this world's goods. You say, 'That's no affair of mine. Am I expected to rescue him from distress with my money?'

If that is your attitude, your heart is empty of God's love, you are not a child of God.

You glory in being a Christian – yes, that is what you are called but not what your deeds answer to. If you don't live like a Christian what is the point of being called one?

Augustine

God, our father and mother

As truly as God is our father, so just as truly is he our mother.

In our father, God Almighty, we have our being; in our merciful mother we are remade and restored. Our fragmented lives are knit together and made perfect man. And by giving and yielding ourselves, through grace, to the Holy Spirit we are made whole.

It is I, the strength and goodness of fatherhood. It is I, the wisdom of motherhood. It is I, the light and grace of holy love. It is I, the Trinity, it is I, the unity. I am the sovereign goodness in all things. It is I who teach you to love. It is I who teach you to desire. It is I who am the reward of all true desiring.

Julian of Norwich

Our true mother, Jesus

A mother's caring is the closest, nearest and surest for it is the truest. This care never might nor could nor should be done fully except by him alone.

As we know, our own mother bore us only into pain and dying. But our true mother Jesus, who is all love, bears us into joy and endless living. Blessed may he be!

A mother feeds her child with her milk, but our beloved mother Jesus feeds us with himself. In tender courtesy he gives us the Blessed Sacrament, the most treasured food of life.

I dare to say full surely, and we should believe it, that there never was so fair a man as he, until his brightness was clouded by trouble and sorrow, Passion and death.

Julian of Norwich

He holds us when we fall

A mother may sometimes let her child fall and suffer in various ways, so that it may learn by its mistakes. But she will never allow any real harm to come to the child because of her love. And though earthly mothers may not be able to prevent their children from dying, our heavenly mother Jesus will never let us, his children, see death. For he is all might, all wisdom, and all love. Blessed may he be!

When we fall he holds us lovingly, and graciously and swiftly raises us.

In all this work he takes the part of a kind nurse who has no other care but the welfare of her child. It is his responsibility to save us, it is his glory to do it, and it is his will we should know it.

Utterly at home, he lives in us for ever.

Julian of Norwich

Trust in God's merciful love

Since the Lord is in heaven I
can only follow him by
traces full of light and
fragrance which he has left
behind him. When I open the
Gospels, I breathe the
fragrance exhaled by the life
of Jesus, and I know which
way to run.

It is to the lowest that I hasten.
I repeat with all confidence the
humble prayer of the publican. Most of all I imitate
the behaviour of Mary Magdalene, for her amazing
– or, rather, loving – audacity which delighted the
heart of Jesus, has cast its spell upon mine.

It is not because I have been preserved from serious
sin that I lift up my heart to God in trust and in love.
I am certain that even if I had on my conscience
every imaginable crime, I should lose nothing of
my confidence, but would throw myself, my heart
broken with sorrow, into the arms of my Saviour.

I remember his love for the prodigal son, I have
heard his words to Mary Magdalene, to the woman
taken in adultery. No – there is no one who could
frighten me, for I know too well what to believe
concerning his mercy and his love.

Thérèse of Lisieux

The sins of the redeemed turned to glory

Also, God showed that sin shall not be a shame to man, but a glory. For just as every sin brings its own suffering, by truth, so every soul that sins earns a blessing by love. And just as many sins are punished with much suffering, because they are so bad, even so they shall be rewarded with many joys in heaven because of the suffering and sorrow they have caused the soul here on earth. For the soul that comes to heaven is so precious to God, and the place so holy, that God in his goodness never allows a soul that reaches heaven to sin without also seeing that those sins have their reward. And the soul is known to God for ever and joyfully restored with great glory.

In this showing my understanding was lifted up to heaven. And then God brought happily to my mind David and others without number from the Old Law, and in the New Law he brought to my mind first Mary Magdalene, Peter and Paul, and those of India, and St John of Beverley – and also others without number. And he showed how the Church on earth knows of them and their sins, and it is no shame to them, but is all turned to their glory.

And so our courteous Lord showed them as an example of how it is in part here on earth and shall be fully in heaven. For there, the mark of sin is turned to honour.

Julian of Norwich

The example of St John of Beverley

As for St John of Beverley, our Lord showed him high in honour to comfort us in our humbleness, and brought to my mind how he is a near neighbour, and well known to us.

And God called him 'St John of Beverley' as plainly as we do, with a glad and happy look, showing that he is a most high saint in God's sight, and a blessed one.

And in this he mentioned that in his youth and early years St John of Beverley was a loyal servant to God, humbly loving and fearing him, and that, nevertheless, God allowed him to fall. But he mercifully upheld him so that he did not perish or lose time.

And afterwards God lifted him up to much more grace. Because of the contrition and humility he had in this life, God has given him many joys in heaven, which go beyond those he would have had if he had not fallen. On earth God shows that this is true by the many miracles that happen continually near his body.

And all this was shown to make us glad and happy in love.

Julian of Norwich

Rest in God

In my soul I heard Jesus say, 'If you will love me with all your heart then I may rest there. If you allow me to rest in your heart on earth then believe me when I tell you that you will rest with me in heaven.'

'I ask no more of you than that you love me as I love you.'

'You know that when you have received me into your soul you are in peace and quiet.'

'I would speak to you more often than you will let me.'

'I would take you by the hand so that people know that you are my friend.'

Margery Kempe

Beasts and saints

We came near to a tree, led by our kindly host, and there we stumbled upon a lion. At the sight of him my guide and I quaked, but the saintly old man went unfaltering on and we followed, timorously enough. The wild beast – you would say it was at the command of God – modestly withdrew a little way and sat down, while the old man plucked the fruit from the lower branches. He held out his hand, full of dates; and up the creature ran and took them as frankly as any tame animal about the house; and when it had finished eating, it went away. We stood watching and trembling; reflecting as well we might what valour of faith was in him and what poverty of spirit in us.

While abba Macarius was praying in his cave in the desert, a hyena suddenly appeared and began to lick his feet and taking him gently by the hem of his tunic, she drew him towards her own cave. He followed her, saying, 'I wonder what this animal wants me to do?' When she had led him to her cave, she went in and brought her cubs which had been born blind. He prayed over them and returned them to the hyena with their sight healed. She in turn, by way of thankoffering, brought the man the huge skin of a ram and laid it at his feet. He smiled at her as if at a kind and sensitive person and taking the skin spread it under him.

The Desert Fathers

Perfect love

The more a soul loves, the
more perfect it is in its love;
hence it follows that the soul
which is already perfect is,
if we may speak in this
manner, all love. All its
actions are love, all its
energies and strength are
occupied in love. It gives up
all it has, like the wise merchant, for this treasure of
love which it finds hidden in God.

The Beloved cares for nothing else but love. The
soul, therefore, anxious to please him perfectly, occu-
pies itself unceasingly in pure love of God.

As the bee draws honey from all plants and makes
use of them only for that end, so the soul most easily
draws the sweetness of love from all that happens to
it. It makes all things subservient to the end of loving
God, whether they are sweet or bitter.

In all its occupations its joy is the love of God.

John of the Cross

The humility of God

God communicates himself to the soul in this interior union with a love so intense that the love of a mother who tenderly caresses her child, the love of a brother or the affection of a friend bears no resemblance to it.

Great is the tenderness and deep the love with which the Eternal Father comforts and exalts the loving soul.

O wonders worthy of awe and reverence! God humbles himself before the soul that he may exalt it, as if he were the servant and the soul his lord. He is as eager to comfort it as if he were a slave and the soul God, so great is the humility and tenderness of God.

In this communication of love he renders in a certain way those services to the soul which he says in the Gospel he will perform for the elect in heaven. 'Amen I say to you, he will gird himself and make them sit down to eat, and passing will minister to them.'

John of the Cross

Like Martha

His Majesty does not lead all
souls by the same way. St
Martha was holy, though we
are never told she was a
contemplative; would you
not be content with
resembling this blessed
woman who deserved to
receive Christ our Lord so
often into her home, where she fed and served him,
and where he ate at her table?

Imagine that this little community is the house of St
Martha where there must be different kinds of
people. Remember that someone must cook the
meals and count yourselves happy in being able to
serve like Martha.

Reflect that true humility consists in being willing
and ready to do what our Lord asks of us. It always
makes us consider ourselves unworthy to be
reckoned among his servants.

Then if contemplation, mental and vocal prayer,
nursing the sick, the work of the house and the most
menial labour, all serve this Guest, why should we
choose to minister to him in one way rather than in
another?

Teresa of Avila

Resignation

O shepherds, you who go
Through the sheepcotes up the hill,
If you should see
Him whom I love
Tell him I languish, suffer and die.

The soul does no more than represent its miseries
and pain to the Beloved, for he who loves wisely does
not wish to ask for what he desires. He is satisfied at
hinting at his necessities so that the Beloved may do
what seems best to him.

There are three reasons for this. First, our Lord
knows what is expedient for us better than we do
ourselves. Secondly, the Beloved is more
compassionate towards us when he sees our necessities and our resignation. Thirdly, we are more secure
against self-love and self-seeking when we represent
our necessity instead of asking for what we think we
need. It is as if the soul said, 'Tell my Beloved to
save me, since I languish and he is my salvation –
that as I am suffering to give me joy, since he alone
is joy; that as I am dying to give me life, since he
alone is my life.'

John of the Cross

The hermit's song

I have a hut in a wood: only my Lord knows it; an ash tree closes it on one side, and a hazel like a great tree by a rath on the other.

The size of my hut, small, not too small, a homestead with familiar paths. From its gable a she-bird sings a sweet song in her thrush's cloak.

A tree of apples of great bounty like a mansion, stout: a pretty bush, thick as a fist, of small hazelnuts, branching and green.

Fair white birds come, herons, seagulls, the sea sings to them, no mournful music; brown grouse from the russet heather.

The sound of the wind against a branching wood, grey cloud, riverfalls, the cry of the swan, delightful music! Beautiful are the pines which make music for me unhindered: through Christ I am no worse off at any time than you.

Though you relish that which you enjoy exceeding all wealth, I am content with that which is given me by my gentle Christ. With no moment of strife, no din of combat such as disturbs you, thankful to the Prince who gives every good to me in my hut.

The Celtic Tradition

The image restored

This shall be for you a luminous sign of the serenity of your soul: when, on examining yourself, you find yourself full of compassion for all humanity, and your heart is afflicted with pity for them, burning as though with fire, without making distinction between one person and another.

When the image of the Father becomes visible in you by means of the continual presence of these things, then you can recognize the measure of your way of life – not from your various labours, but from the transformation which your understanding receives.

The body is then likely to be bathed in tears, as the intellect gazes on things spiritual.

Isaac of Syria

Singlemindedness

The soul, in the courage of its love, glories in what ministers to the Beloved, in that it has done anything for him, and is lost to the things of the world.

The soul remembers the words of the Bridegroom in the Gospel, 'No man can serve two masters', and therefore in order not to lose God, he loses all that is not God. He who truly loves makes shipwreck of himself in all else, that he may more easily gain the object of his love.

The soul loses itself, making no account whatever of itself but of the Beloved, resigning itself freely into his hands without any self-seeking. It holds everything of no value unless it serves the Beloved.

He that loves God seeks neither gain nor reward, but only to lose all, even himself.

John of the Cross

Advice to married people

'Marriage is a great sacrament: I speak in Christ and in the Church' (Ephesians 5:32). It is honourable to all, in all, and in everything, that is, in all its parts. The unmarried should esteem it in humility. It is as holy to the poor as to the rich. Its institution, its end, its purpose, its form and its matter are all holy.

It greatly concerns the public welfare that the sanctity of marriage, which is the source of all its well-being, should be preserved inviolate.

I exhort married persons to have that mutual love which is so earnestly enjoined by the Holy Spirit in Scripture.

The first result of such love is the indissoluble union of your hearts. This spiritual union of the heart, with its affections and love, is stronger than that of more bodily union.

The second result of this love is absolute faithfulness.

The third end of marriage is the birth and bringing-up of children.

Love and faithfulness always breed confidence.

Francis de Sales

Self-surrender to love

Do not think I am overwhelmed with consolations. Far from it! My joy consists in being deprived of all joy here on earth. Jesus does not guide me openly; I neither see nor hear him. Nor is it through books that I learn, for I do not understand what I read. Yet at times I am consoled by some chance words, such as the following which I read after a meditation passed in utter dryness: the Lord said to St Margaret Mary: 'Here is the master I give you. He will teach you all. I wish to make you read in the Book of Life in which is contained the science of love.'

The science of love – these words re-echo in my soul. I wish for no other knowledge, and like the spouse in the Canticle of Canticles, 'having given up all the substance of my house for love, I reckon it as nothing' (Song 8:7). I understand clearly that through love alone can we become pleasing to God, and my sole ambition is to acquire it.

Jesus points out to me the only way which leads to Love's furnace – that way is self-surrender – it is the confidence of the little child who sleeps without fear in its father's arms. The Spirit of Love declares: 'To him that is little, mercy is granted' (Wisdom 6:7). In his name, too, the prophet Isaiah foretells how on the last day the Lord 'will feed his flock like a shepherd; he will gather together the lambs in his arms, and shall take them to his bosom' (Isaiah 40:11).

Thérèse of Lisieux

Bound to him in love

I set my eyes on the same cross that had comforted me before. I set my tongue to speak of Christ's Passion and to recite the creed. I set my heart on God with all my trust and with all my might.

It is God's will that I should see myself as bound to him in love as if all that he has done he has done for me alone. And so should every soul think inwardly of its lover.

He wills that our hearts should be lifted high above the depths of earthly and vain sorrows, and rejoice in him.

He loves us and enjoys us, and so he wills that we love him and enjoy him, and firmly trust him; and all shall be well.

Julian of Norwich

The hope of salvation

My mind was lifted up to heaven and I saw our Lord as a lord in his own house where he had called his much-loved friends and servants to a banquet. I saw that the Lord did not sit in one place but ranged throughout the house, filling it with joy and gladness.

Completely relaxed and courteous, he was himself the happiness and peace of his dear friends, his beautiful face radiating measureless love like a marvellous symphony; and it was that wonderful face shining with the beauty of God that filled that heavenly place with joy and light.

If I look at myself I am nothing. But if I look at us all I am hopeful; for I see the unity of love among all my fellow-Christians. In this unity lies our salvation.

Because of these revelations I am not good, but only if I love God better. If you love God better than I do, by that much you are better than I.

Julian of Norwich

Advice to a woman in the world

This is what you should do during the time you spend in the country. If you faithfully follow my counsels they will sanctify this time of rest and make it bear fruit.

Approach the sacraments as often as you are allowed to do so.

Offer to God each morning the recreations of the day and with them the different pains, both exterior and interior, with which he is pleased in his goodness to season them, and say from time to time: 'Blessed be God in all things and for all things; Lord, may your holy will be done.'

In the course of the day occupy yourself about things that are necessary, and that obedience requires of you, and which divine Providence has marked out for you.

Be careful to drop vain and useless thoughts directly you are conscious of them, but quietly, without effort or violence.

Above everything drop all anxious thoughts, abandoning to divine Providence all that might become a subject of preoccupation for you.

Jean-Pierre de Caussade

Further advice to the same

As you are less busy than others, employ more of your time in reading good books, and in order to make this more efficacious, set about it in this way:

Begin by placing yourself in the presence of God and by begging his help.

Read quietly, slowly, word for word, to enter into the subject more with the heart than with the mind.

At the end of each paragraph that contains a complete meaning, stop for the time it would take you to recite an 'Our Father', or even a little longer, to assimilate what you have read, or to rest and remain peacefully before God.

Should this peace and rest last for a longer time, it will be all the better; but when you feel that your mind wanders, resume your reading, and continue thus, frequently renewing these same pauses.

Nothing need prevent you from continuing the same method, if you find it useful to your soul, during the time you have fixed for meditation.

Jean-Pierre de Caussade

The joy of God's love

Whoever loves another does so according to his own attributes and properties. Therefore, since the Lord the Bridegroom is within you and is all-powerful, he gives you power and loves you with the same.

Since he is wise he loves you with wisdom.
Since he is good he loves you with goodness.
Since he is holy he loves you with holiness.
Since he is just he loves you with justice.
Since he is merciful he loves you with mercy.
Since he is compassionate and understanding
   he loves you with gentleness and sweetness.

He loves you with the greatest humility and the deepest respect, making himself your equal and making you his equal. He joyfully reveals his face to you, saying to you, 'I am yours, completely yours. And my happiness is to be who I am so that I may give myself to you and be all yours.'

John of the Cross

Prayer

Some monks came to see abba Lucius and they said to him, 'We do not work with our hands; we obey Paul's command and pray without ceasing.' The old man said, 'Do you not eat or sleep?' They said, 'Yes, we do.' He said, 'Who prays for you while you are asleep? . . . Excuse me, brothers, but you do not practise what you claim. I will show you how I pray without ceasing, though I work with my hands.'

'With God's help, I collect a few palm-leaves and sit down and weave them, saying, "Have mercy upon me, O God, after thy great goodness; according to the multitude of thy mercies do away with mine offences." ' He said to them, 'Is this prayer or not?' They said, 'Yes, it is.'

And he continued, 'When I have worked and prayed in my heart all day, I make about sixteen pence. Two of these I put outside my door and with the rest I buy food. And he who finds the two coins outside the door prays for me while I eat and sleep. And so by the help of God I pray without ceasing.'

The Desert Fathers

What the world may say

Directly people of the world perceive that you seek a life of prayer, they will launch their jeering and slander at you. The most ill-natured will declare your altered ways hypocrisy or affectation; they will say that the world has slighted you, and so you have rejected it, and turned to God. They will tell you that you will grow morbid, lose your position in the world, that your home affairs will suffer, that in the world we must do as the world does, that we can be saved without extravagances.

But these are foolishnesses, because those who utter them are not really concerned for you. Whereas people can spend all night at cards or dancing, and their friends are not disturbed, if we devote an hour to meditation or get up early to prepare for Holy Communion there is an outcry.

The world is an unjust judge, indulging its own children and being harsh towards the children of God.

Francis de Sales

Humility is the foundation of prayer

God is greatly pleased when
he beholds a soul in its
humility making his Son a
Mediator between itself and
him, and yet loving him so
much as to confess its own
unworthiness, even when he
would raise it up to the
highest contemplation, and
saying with St Peter: 'Go away from me, O Lord,
for I am a sinful man.'

I know this by experience; it was thus that God
directed my soul. I have understood that the whole
foundation of prayer must be laid in humility, and
that the more a soul humbles itself in prayer, the
more God lifts it up.

I do not remember that he ever showed me any of
those marvellous mercies of which I shall speak at
any other time than when I was as one brought to
nothing, by seeing how wicked I was.

Moreover His Majesty contrived to make me understand matters that helped me to know myself, but
which I could never have even imagined of myself.

Teresa of Avila

On fasting

I am to show in what manner we are to fast, that it may be an acceptable service unto the Lord. And, first, let it be done unto the Lord, with our eye singly fixed on him. Let our intention herein be this, and this alone, to glorify our Father which is in heaven. Let us beware of mocking God, of turning our fast, as well as our prayers, into an abomination unto the Lord, by the mixture of any temporal view, particularly by seeking the praise of men.

Let us beware, secondly, of fancying that we *merit* anything of God by our fasting. We cannot be too often warned of this, inasmuch as a desire to 'establish our own righteousness', to procure salvation of debt and not of grace, is so deeply rooted in all our hearts. Fasting is only a way which God hath ordained, wherein we wait for his unmerited mercy, and wherein, without any desert of ours, he hath promised freely to give us his blessing.

Not that we are to imagine that performing the bare outward act will receive any blessing from God. Let us take care to afflict our souls as well as our bodies. Let every season, either of public or private fasting, be a season of exercising all those holy affections which are implied in a broken and contrite heart.

John Wesley

Unbelief or half-belief

In the very act of affirming my faith, my God and Father suffers me to be thrown into prison, drowned, beheaded. It is then my faith falters, and in a moment of weakness I cry, 'Who knows whether it is really true?' . . .

At such a moment we must say, 'Let go of everything in which I have trusted'. And then turn to God and say, 'Lord, you alone give help and comfort. You have said that you would help me. I believe your word. O my God and Lord, I have heard from you a joyful and comforting word. I hold to that word. I know you cannot lie to me. No matter how you may appear to me, you will keep the word you have promised. That, and nothing else.'

The story of the Canaanite woman* shows us how deeply God can hide his face from us, and how we should not judge God according to our subjective feeling and thinking about him, but *only* in accordance with his word. All Christ's answers sounded like 'No!', though he pronounced no final 'No!' Yet, all his answers sounded more like 'No!' than 'Yes!' Our hearts feel the same in the hour of trial. We see nothing but a plain 'No!' Therefore, underneath and beyond the 'No!' grasp the deeply hidden 'Yes!' Hold on, as the woman did, to God's word.

Martin Luther

* Mt 15:27–28.

Our Lady

Mary, the Mother of God, rested in my soul and said, 'I bring you greetings from my son Jesus and all the angels and saints in heaven. I will be a mother to you, to teach you how to please God.'

'Do not be afraid to accept the gifts my son will give you.'

'If you would share in our love you must also share in our sorrow.'

Glorious Queen of heaven, anyone who has you for a friend will be greatly blessed, for when you pray, the whole company of heaven prays with you.

Margery Kempe

You are my heaven

And then I wanted to look away from the cross, and I dared not. For I knew well that while I looked at the cross I was safe and sure. I did not want to put my soul in peril, for there was no safety from the terrors of devils, except for the cross.

Then I heard a word in my ear that kindly said to me: 'Look up to heaven to his Father.'

Then I saw clearly by faith that there was nothing between the cross and heaven that could have done me any harm. Either I had to look up or to answer.

I answered inwardly with all my soul's strength and said: 'No, I cannot, for you are my heaven.' This I said because I did not want to look away – for I had rather have borne that pain until the Day of Judgement than come to heaven any other way than through him. For I knew well that he who bound me so fast could unbind me when he chose.

So I was taught to choose Jesus for my heaven, though I saw him only in pain at that time. I wanted no other heaven than Jesus, who shall be my joy when I come there.

Julian of Norwich

Not to advance is to go back

[Brother Lawrence continued]:

I say again, let us enter into ourselves. Time presses, there is no room for delay; each must answer for himself. You, I believe, have taken such effectual measures that you will not be surprised. I commend you for it; it is the one thing needful.

We must, nevertheless, always work at it, for, in the spiritual life, not to advance is to go back.

But those whose spirits are stirred by the breath of the Holy Spirit go forward even in sleep.

If the vessel of our soul is still tossed with winds and storms, let us awake the Lord, who reposes in it, and he will quickly calm the sea.

I have taken the liberty to impart to you these good thoughts, that you may compare them with your own. It will serve again to rekindle and inflame them, if by misfortune (which God forbid, for it would be indeed a great misfortune) they should be, though never so little, cooled.

Let us then both recall our early fervour . . . . I will pray for you; do you pray instantly for me.

Brother Lawrence

Hope

Through hope we already dwell in heaven. Our cause rests in the hands of him who distinctly tells us, 'No one can snatch them out of my hand.'* He said more: 'The gates of hell shall not prevail against my Church.'†

If we go under, then Christ, who is the almighty ruler of this world, must himself go under with us. Even if the cause of the Reformation were to collapse, I would much rather go to rack and ruin with Christ than stand triumphant with Caesar!

The one thing necessary is to believe, and to pray with complete confidence in the name of Christ, that God will give us the strength necessary. Without our help, counsel, thought or effort, he himself alone has brought forth his Kingdom, advanced it and preserved it to this day. I have not the slightest doubt that he will consummate it without our advice or assistance.‡

God, in his gracious kindness, has given us in the vale of this world his holy, precious word, and his own dear Son . . . He will continue as God and Creator long after we are dead and gone. He was there before we appeared on the scene. To the end of time he will continue to gather to himself a little flock, and he will uphold it.

Martin Luther

* Jn 10:28.   † Mt 16:18.   ‡ 2 Tm 1:12; Ep 2:20.

God's cure for our sins

God showed me that we suffer from two kinds of sickness. One is the impatience or sloth whereby our pains and troubles press heavily upon us; the other is despair and fearfulness . . . These are the two evils which most trouble and buffet us, as our Lord showed me. And he would have us cured of them.

I speak of those men and women who, for God's love, hate sin and turn themselves to do God's will. These are the sins we are most likely to fall into because of our inward blindness and earthly sadness. And so it is God's will that we should recognize them and turn our backs on them as we do on other sins.

Our Lord himself gives us great help in curing these sins by showing us his patience in his hard and grievous Passion; and also the joy and delight he had in that Passion, for love. So he shows us by his example that we should bear our pains gladly and wisely. To him this brings great happiness, and to us enduring gain.

He wants us to see and enjoy everything in love.

Julian of Norwich

God courteously forgives

Some of us believe that God is all-powerful and may do everything; and that he is all-wise and can do everything; but as for believing that he is all love and will do everything, there we hold back. In my view nothing hinders God's lovers more than the failure to understand this.

For when we begin to hate sin and to mend our ways by the guidance of Holy Church, yet a fear still lingers and holds us back. This is because we see ourselves and the sins we have done before, and some of us see the sins we sin each day . . . And looking at this makes us so sad and worried that we can scarcely find comfort.

And sometimes we take this fear to be humility, but it is a wicked blindness and weakness. And we cannot scotch it as we do a sin which we recognize, because it springs from the devil's work. And it contradicts truth. For, of all the properties of the blessed Trinity, it is God's will that the one we should have most faith and delight in, is love.

For love makes strength and wisdom gentle to us. For as by his courtesy God forgives our sin when we repent, even so he wills that we should forgive our sin, and so give up our senseless worrying and faithless fear.

Julian of Norwich

Three kinds of martyrdom

Now there are three kinds of martyrdom which are counted as a cross to man, that is to say, white martyrdom, and green martyrdom, and red martyrdom.

This is the white martyrdom to man, when he separates for the sake of God from everything he loves, although he suffer fasting or labour thereat.

This is the green martyrdom to him, when by means of them (fasting and penance) he separates from his desires, or suffers toil in penance and repentance.

This is the red martyrdom to him, endurance of a cross or destruction for Christ's sake, as has happened to the apostles in the persecution of the wicked and in teaching the law of God.

These three kinds of martyrdom are comprised in the carnal ones who resort to good repentance, who separate from their desires, who pour forth their blood in fasting and in labour for Christ's sake.

The Celtic Tradition

One way, one truth and one life

Give up yourselves to the
meek and humble spirit of the
holy Jesus, the overcomer of
all fire and pride and wrath.
This is the one way, the one
truth and the one life. There
is no other open door into
the sheepfold of God.
Everything else is the
working of the devil in the fallen nature of man.

Humility must sow the seed, or there can be no
reaping in heaven. Look not at pride only as an
unbecoming temper; nor at humility only as a decent
virtue; for the one is death and the other is life; the
one is hell and the other is all heaven.

So much as you have of pride, so much you have of
the fallen angel alive in you; so much as you have of
true humility, so much you have of the Lamb of God
within you. 'Learn of me for I am meek and lowly
of heart.' If this lesson is unlearnt, we must be said
to have left our Master, as those disciples did who
went back and walked no more with him.

William Law

True humility flows from God alone

Let us look first at the virtue of humility.

It is imperfect when it originates from anything other than God, even though God be the chief source. It is perfect when it flows from God himself.

In itself humility is a true knowledge and awareness of oneself as one really is. It is undoubtedly true that if any man could see and know himself as he is, he would be truly humble.

There are two sources from which humility springs. The first is the depravity and wretchedness and weakness of man, into which state he has fallen through sin. In some degree he must always be aware of this throughout his life, however holy he may be.

The second source is the overwhelming love and goodness of God himself, at the sight of which nature trembles, learned men are fools and saints and angels blinded.

The second is perfect; and that is because it will last for ever.

Author of 'The Cloud of Unknowing'

The nature of charity

Charity means nothing else but to love God for himself above all creatures, and to love one's fellowmen for God's sake even as one loves oneself.

It is entirely right and fitting that in this work God should be loved for himself and above all creation. For, as has been noted earlier, the essential nature of this work is nothing other than a naked intent directed to God for his sake only.

I call it a naked intent because in this work the perfect apprentice does not ask for remission of pain, nor for a greater reward, nor in short for anything but God himself.

It is even true that he neither takes notice nor considers whether he is in pain or in joy, but is concerned simply that the will of God whom he loves is fulfilled.

Thus, in this work God is perfectly loved for himself, and above all creation. In it the perfect worker may not allow the memory of the holiest creature God ever made to have any share in what is being done.

Author of 'The Cloud of Unknowing'

The Divine Eagle

If you remain deaf to the plaintive cries of this feeble creature, should you hide yourself, then I am content to remain numb with cold, my wings bedraggled – and once more I would rejoice.

I am happy to feel myself so small and frail in your presence, and my heart is at peace . . . for I know that all the eagles of heaven have pity on me and that they guard and defend me, putting to flight the vulture-like temptations which would destroy me.

I do not fear these temptations because I am not destined to be their prey, but the prey of the Divine Eagle.

Eternal Word, Saviour! You are the Divine Eagle whom I love. You draw me. You came into this land of exile, willing to suffer and to die, in order to carry away every single soul and plunge it into the very heart of the Trinity – love's eternal home.

You returned to your realm of light, and still remain hidden here to nourish us, in our vale of tears, with Holy Communion. Forgive me if I tell you that your love reaches even to madness. At the sight of such folly, surely you expect my own heart to leap up to you? My trust can know no bounds.

Thérèse of Lisieux

The folly of love

I know well that for your sake the saints have made themselves foolish – being 'eagles', they have done great things. Too little for such deeds, my folly lies in the hope that your love will accept me, and in my confidence that the angels and saints will help me to fly to you.

As long as you will it, I shall remain with my gaze fixed on you, for I long to be fascinated by your divine eyes, to be a prey to your love.

I am filled with the hope that one day you will swoop down upon me and bear me away to the source of all love . . . that you will plunge me into its glowing abyss.

Jesus, I want to tell all little souls of the wonder of your love. If by any chance you could find a soul weaker than mine, which would abandon itself in perfect trust to your infinite mercy, I feel you would take delight in loading it with still greater favours.

Where do these desires to make known the secrets of your love come from? You alone can have taught them to me. You alone can reveal them to others. I ask you to look upon a vast number of little souls; choose in this world a legion of little people worthy of your love.

Thérèse of Lisieux

A conversion

The very toys of toys and vanities of vanities still held me; they plucked at the garment of my flesh and whispered softly, 'Will you cast us off for ever? And from that moment shall we no longer be with you – for ever?', and I hesitated, for a strong habit said to me, 'Do you think you can live without them?'

But continence said to me, 'Why do you rely on yourself and so waver? Cast yourself upon him, fear not, he will not withdraw himself and let you fall; he will receive you and heal you.'

So I rose and, throwing myself down under a certain fig tree, wept bitterly in contrition of heart. Suddenly I heard from a neighbouring house the voice of a child, singing over and over again, 'Take up and read, take up and read.'

Checking my weeping I got up and went back to where I had been sitting, and had laid down the volume of the apostle, and read the first passage which met my eyes: 'Not in rioting and drunkenness, not in impurity and wantonness, not in strife and envy; but put on the Lord Jesus Christ, and make no provision for the flesh, to fulfil its lusts.'

I needed to read no further, for suddenly, as it were by a light infused into my heart, all darkness vanished away.

Augustine

Beatitude

The end of all our action is contemplation as it will be the everlasting perfection of everyone, for God said to his servant Moses, 'I am he who is', and it is him that we shall contemplate in eternal life. For the Lord said, 'This is eternal life: to know thee the one true God, and Jesus Christ whom thou hast sent.'

This will come to pass when the Lord comes and the darkness and corruption of our mortality vanish. That will be our tomorrow, when we shall not look for anything else except that joy which we now hope for. We shall not seek greater happiness, for there will be none.

We shall see the Father and that will suffice us. Philip realized this when he asked it of the Lord, but he did not understand that he could have said, 'Lord, show us thyself and it is enough', and so the Lord said, 'He who sees me, sees the Father'.

Contemplation is the reward of that faith which purifies our hearts (and it is the pure of heart who will see God). So it does not matter whether we say, 'Show us the Father', or 'Show us the Son': we cannot be shown one without the other, since with the Holy Spirit they are one. Beloved, realize that the joy of all joys will be to delight in the Trinity in whose image we have been created.

Augustine

Martha and Mary

The Lord said, 'I will see you again, and your hearts will rejoice, and no one shall take your joy away.' Mary prefigured that joy when she sat at the Lord's feet listening to what he said.

She was silent, doing no work, she cleaved to the truth as far as can be in this life, yet it is only a foreshadowing of the joy that will last for ever.

Her sister Martha was occupied with work that has to be done, but which, however good and useful, will pass away when we come to eternal rest. So the Lord said, 'Mary has chosen the best part, which shall not be taken from her.' He did not say that Martha's part was bad, only that the one which would not be taken away was the better.

For example, the work of looking after the needy will pass away, when there is no more poverty. But it is not the transitory good works that will gain us eternal rest. In contemplating God each of us will find all that we desire, for he will be all in all when we see and possess him; that is why his Holy Spirit in our hearts makes us pray: 'One thing have I asked, this I have longed for: to dwell for ever in the Lord's house and contemplate his love.'

Augustine

Seeking God only

[My second conversation with Brother Lawrence took place on 28 September 1666. In the course of our talk he said]:

That he had always been governed by love, without selfish views, and without concerning himself whether he would be lost or saved; and that having resolved to make the love of God the *end* of all his actions, he had good reason to be well satisfied with his method.

He was pleased when he could take up a straw from the ground for the love of God, seeking him only, and nothing else, not even his gifts.

In order to form a habit of conversing with God continually, and referring all we do to him, we must first apply to him with some diligence.

After a little care we should find his love inwardly excite us to it without any difficulty.

Brother Lawrence

The power of prayer

Once a person has become humble, straightaway mercy encircles and embraces him; and once mercy has approached, immediately his heart becomes aware of God helping him, since he discovers a certain powerful assurance stirring within him.

When someone has become aware of the coming of divine help, and that it is this which aids and assists him, then at once his heart is filled with faith, and from this he understands that prayer is: the haven of help, the fountainhead of salvation, a treasury of assurance, a saving anchor in time of storm, an illumination to those in darkness, a staff for the weak, a shelter in time of trials, a source of recovery at the time of sickness, a shield of deliverance in war, an arrow sharpened in face of enemies.

Having found an entry to all these excellent things through prayer, henceforth that person will rejoice in the prayer of faith, his heart exulting in confidence – no longer blindly, or through lip-service only, as had previously been the case. Once aware of this, he has acquired prayer in his soul, like a treasure. Out of the joy he experiences he will change the direction of his prayer, turning it into utterance of thanksgiving. This corresponds to what was said by Evagrius, wise among the saints and ready for every eventuality, namely that 'Prayer is joy which gives rise to thanksgiving'.

Isaac of Syria

God speaks in secret

If a soul is seeking God, its
Beloved is seeking it still
more.

When the soul reflects that
God is the guide of its blind
self, then its main
preoccupation will be to see
that it sets no obstacle in the
way of its guide, the Holy Spirit, upon the road by
which God is leading it.

The soul then has to walk with loving advertence to
God, without making specific acts, and exerting no
effort on its own part. It must keep a simple, pure
and loving awareness, like one who gazes with the
awareness of love.

The soul must be attached to nothing, whether of
sense or spirit, which would introduce noise into the
deep silence. There the voice of God speaks to the
heart in this secret place, in utmost peace and
tranquillity.

John of the Cross

Darkness tends towards light

I see the black cloud
Now about to flee,
And the wind from the north
Is veering just a little;
After a great storm, there will shortly come
Pleasant weather upon my poor soul.

Nothing will remain long
Of the black stormy night;
Long ages have not been appointed
For anyone to carry the cross;
The glad dawn that shines yonder
Says that a fine morning is on the way.

I see the sunlight
On the hills of my Father's house,
Showing me the foundation
Of my free salvation;
That my name is up there on the books of heaven,
And that there is nothing that can blot it out.

Sweet as the honeycomb,
And nourishing and healing,
Are all heaven's chastisements
And the strokes of my Father's rod:
Each cross, each woe, each strong wind
Ripens saints for heaven.

The Celtic Tradition

God is for all

There was an old man living in the desert who served God for many years and he said, 'Lord, let me know if I have pleased you.' He saw an angel who said to him, 'You have not yet become like the gardener in such and such a place.' The old man marvelled and said, 'I will go off to the city to see both him and what it is that he does that surpasses all my work and toil of all these years.' . . .

So he went to the city and asked the gardener about his way of life . . . When they were getting ready to eat in the evening, the old man heard people in the streets singing songs, for the cell of the gardener was in a public place. Therefore the old man said to him, 'Brother, wanting as you do to live according to God, how do you remain in this place and not be troubled when you hear them singing these songs?'

The man said, 'I tell you, abba, I have never been troubled or scandalized.' When he heard this the old man said, 'What, then, do you think in your heart when you hear these things?' And he replied, 'That they are all going into the Kingdom.' When he heard this, the old man marvelled and said, 'This is the practice which surpasses my labour of all these years.'

The Desert Fathers

Here today and gone tomorrow

Wherever the soul of man turns, unless it turns to you it clasps sorrow to its heart. Even if it clings to what is lovely, if this loveliness is outside God, it has clung to sorrow, for these beautiful things would not exist without you. Like the sun, they rise and set: they have their beginning and then they grow old and die.

Let me praise you for these things, my God who made them all, but do not let the love of them be like glue to fix them to my soul.

In these things there is nowhere to rest, because they do not last, they pass away beyond the reach of our senses. Indeed, we cannot lay firm hold on them even when they are with us.

In this world one thing passes away, and another takes its place. But does the Word of God pass away? Make your dwelling in him. Entrust to him whatever you have, for all you possess is from him. In him is the peace that cannot be disturbed, and he will not withhold himself from your love if you do not withhold your love from him.

Augustine

Abandonment to be embraced not feared

Those who have gauged the depths of their own nothingness can no longer retain any kind of confidence in themselves, nor trust in any way to their works in which they can discover nothing but misery, self-love and corruption.

This absolute distrust and complete disregard of self is the source from which alone flow those delightful consolations of souls wholly abandoned to God, and form their unalterable peace, holy joy and immovable confidence in God only.

Oh! if you but knew the gift of God, the value, merit, power, peace and holy assurance of salvation hidden in this state of abandonment, you would soon be delivered from all your fears and anxieties.

But you imagine you will be lost directly you think of abandoning yourself; and yet the most efficacious means of salvation is to practise this total and perfect abandonment.

I have never yet come across any who have so set themselves against making this act of abandonment to God, as you. Nevertheless, you will necessarily have to come to it, at least at the hour of death. Everyone is absolutely compelled then to abandon self to the very great mercy of God.

Jean-Pierre de Caussade

Faith in Christ alone

'But', you say, 'if I had lived a holy life and performed some good works, I might think myself authorized to practise this abandonment, and to divest myself of my fears.' An illusion, my dear sister. Such language can only have been inspired by your unhappy self-love, which desires to be able to trust entirely to itself, whereas you ought to place your confidence only in God and in the infinite merits of Jesus Christ.

You have never really thoroughly fathomed this essential point but have always stopped short to examine into your fears and doubts instead of rising above them, and throwing yourself heart and soul into the hands of God, and upon his fatherly breast.

In other words, you always want to have a distinct assurance based on yourself in order to abandon yourself better. Most certainly this is anything but an abandonment to God in complete confidence in him only, but, rather, a secret desire of being able to depend on yourself before abandoning yourself to his infinite goodness.

This is to act like a state criminal who, before abandoning himself to the clemency of the king, wishes to be assured of his pardon. Can this be called depending on God, hoping only in God? Judge for yourself.

Jean-Pierre de Caussade

Two objections answered

But are we not commanded to think of ourselves, to enter into ourselves, to watch over ourselves? Yes, certainly, when beginning to enter the service of God in order to detach ourselves from the world, to forsake exterior objects, to correct the bad habits we have contracted; but, afterwards, we must forget ourselves to think only of God, forsake ourselves to belong to God alone.

But as for you, you wish to remain always wrapped up in yourself, in your so-called spiritual interests; and God, to draw you out of this last resource of self-love, allows you to find nothing in yourself but a source of fears, doubts, uncertainty, trouble, anxiety and depression, as though this God of goodness said by this: 'Forget yourself and you will find in me only, peace, spiritual joy, calmness and an absolute assurance of salvation.'

But again you say: 'In this forgetfulness of self, far from correcting myself of my sins and imperfections, I do not even know them.' An error! An illusion! Ignorance! Never can you more clearly detect your faults than in the clear light of the presence of God.

In this way also, better than in any other, all our defects and imperfections are gradually consumed like straw in a fire.

Jean-Pierre de Caussade

Appearances

Do not judge a person by their outward appearance. Only God knows what is in their soul.

Jesus said, 'I thank you because you wish that all people should love me and that they would give as much time and thought to loving me as they do to earning a living.'

'I know that you have wished for great wealth so that you could give it away, in my name. I accept your thoughts as the gifts you would have given.'

In my heart I said, 'I wish I were as deserving of your love as Mary Magdalene.' Our Lord answered, 'I love you just as well and I give you the same peace as I gave her. No saint in heaven minds when I love a person on earth as much as I love them.'

Margery Kempe

Every man's life is a continual state of prayer

Every man's life is a continual state of prayer; he is no moment free from it, nor can possibly be so.

For all our natural tempers, be they what they will, ambition, covetousness, selfishness, worldly-mindedness, pride, envy, hatred, malice or any other lust whatever, are all of them in reality only so many different kinds and forms of a spirit of prayer which is inseparable from the heart as weight is from the body.

For every natural temper is nothing else but a manifestation of the desire and prayer of the heart, and shows us how it works and wills. And as the heart works and wills, such and no other is its prayer.

If, therefore, the working desire of the heart is not habitually turned towards God, if this is not our spirit of prayer, we are necessarily in a state of prayer towards something else that carries us from God and brings all kind of evil into us. Pray we must, as sure as our heart is alive; and therefore when the state of our heart is not a spirit of prayer to God, we pray without ceasing to some or other part of the creation.

William Law

The sins of others

The soul which would remain in peace when another's sin comes to mind, must fly as from the pains of hell, asking for God's protection and help.

Looking at another's sin clouds the eyes of the soul, hiding for the time being the fair beauty of God unless we look upon this sinner with contrition with him, compassion on him, and a holy longing to God for him. Otherwise it must harm and disquiet and hinder the soul that looks on these sins.

He who is highest and closest to God may see himself – and needs to do so – as a sinner like me; and I who am the least and lowest who shall be saved, may be comforted with him who is the highest.

I saw that all compassion to one's fellow-Christians, exercised in love, is a mark of Christ's indwelling.

Julian of Norwich

All manner of thing shall be well

One time, our good Lord said: 'All things shall be well.' And another time, he said: 'You shall see for yourself that all manner of thing shall be well.' The soul understood several things from these sayings.

One was this: that it is his will that we should understand that not only does he take care of great and noble things but also of little and humble things, simple and small – both one and the other. And this is what he means when he says: 'All manner of thing shall be well.' For he wants us to understand that the smallest thing shall not be forgotten.

Something else I understood was this: that we see such evil deeds done, and such great harm caused by them, that it seems to us that it is impossible that any good deed should come out of them. And we look on them, sorrowing and mourning over them, so that we cannot find rest in the joyful sight of God, as we ought to.

The trouble is this – that the range of our thinking is now so blinkered, so little and small, that we cannot see the high, wonderful wisdom and the power and goodness of the blessed Trinity. And this is what he means when he says: 'You shall see for yourself that all manner of thing shall be well.' It was as if he said: 'Have faith, and have trust, and at the last day you shall see it all transformed into great joy.'

Julian of Norwich

Poverty of spirit in the midst of wealth

'Blessed are the poor in spirit, for theirs is the kingdom of heaven' (Matthew 5:3). He is rich in spirit whose heart is in his riches and whose riches fill his heart. He is poor in spirit who does not have riches in his heart or his heart in riches.

Your heart should be open only to heaven and impenetrable to riches and earthly things; if you possess them, be poor in the midst of wealth, and master of its riches. Beware of losing the spirit of holiness in the good things of the world, but let it be superior always, not in them but over them.

You may possess riches without being poisoned by them, if you have them in your house or in your purse, and not in your heart, being rich in substance but poor in spirit.

It is a great happiness for a Christian to be actually rich, but poor in spirit, for he can use wealth and its advantages in this world, and yet have the merit of poverty as regards the next.

Francis de Sales

The role of reason

Let reason do all that reason can. Employ it as far as it will go. But, at the same time, acknowledge that it is utterly incapable of giving either faith, or hope, or love, and consequently of producing either real virtue or substantial happiness.

Expect these from a higher source, even from the Father of the spirits of all flesh. Seek and receive them, not as your own acquisition, but as the gift of God. Lift up your hearts to him who 'giveth to all men liberally and upbraideth not'.

He alone can give that faith which is 'the evidence' and conviction 'of things not seen'. He alone can 'beget you unto a lively hope' of an inheritance eternal in the heavens; and he alone can 'shed his love abroad in your heart by the Holy Ghost given unto you'.

Ask, therefore, and it shall be given you! Cry unto him, and you shall not cry in vain! So shall you be living witnesses that wisdom, holiness and happiness are one, are inseparably united and are indeed the beginning of that eternal life which God hath given us in his Son.

John Wesley

The cross

The cross teaches us to believe in hope even when there is no hope. The wisdom of the cross is deeply hidden in a profound mystery. In fact, there is no other way to heaven than taking up the cross of Christ. On account of this we must beware that the active life with its good works, and the contemplative life with its speculations, do not lead us astray. Both are most attractive and yield peace of mind, but for that very reason they hide real dangers, unless they are tempered by the cross and disturbed by adversaries. The cross is the surest path of all. Blessed is the man who understands this truth.

It is a matter of necessity that we be destroyed and rendered formless, so that Christ may be formed within us, and Christ alone be in us . . . Real mortifications do not happen in lonely places away from the society of other human beings. No! They happen in the home, the market place, in secular life . . . 'Being conformed to Christ' is not within our powers to achieve. It is God's gift, not our own work.

He who is not *crucianus*, if I may coin a word, is not *Christianus*: in other words, he who does not bear his cross is no Christian, for he is not like his Master, Jesus Christ.

Martin Luther

Passing the light

Some time ago I was
watching the flicker, almost
imperceptible, of a tiny
night-light. One of the sisters
came up, and having lit her
own candle in the dying
flame, passed it round to
light the candles of the
others. And the thought
came to me: 'Who dares
glory in their own good
works? It needs but one faint spark to set the world
on fire.'

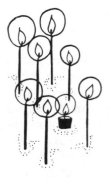

We come in touch with burning and shining lights,
set high on the candlestick of the Church, and we
think we are receiving from them grace and light.
But from where do they borrow their fire?

Very possibly from the prayers of some devout and
hidden soul whose inward shining is not apparent to
human eyes – some soul of unrecognized virtue, and
in her own sight of little worth: a dying flame!

What mysteries we shall one day see unveiled! I have
often thought that perhaps I owe all the graces with
which I am laden to some little soul whom I shall
know only in heaven.

Thérèse of Lisieux

Doubt and uncertainty

God is invisible, inscrutable, incomprehensible, and so on . . . Give up all such speculating, which is utterly unrelated to the word of God anyhow. God is saying to you, From the unrevealed God I shall become your own revealed God: I shall incarnate my own beloved Son . . . 'This is my beloved Son. Hear you him.'* Behold his death, his cross, his Passion. See him hanging on his mother's breast, and hanging on the cross. What Christ says and does, you may be sure of. 'No man cometh to the Father but by me.'† 'He that hath seen me hath seen the Father.'‡ What God is saying to you is this: 'Here in Christ you have me, here in Christ you will see me.'

If you want to escape from despair and hatred of God, let speculation go. Begin with God *from the bottom upwards, not from the top downwards.* In other words, begin with Christ incarnate, and with your own terrible original sin. There is no other way. Otherwise, you will remain a doubter for the rest of your life.

At all costs cling to the revealed God. Allow no one to take the child Jesus from you. Hold fast to Christ, and you will *never* be lost. God the Father longs for you. God the Son wishes to be your Saviour, your Liberator. In this kind and lovely manner has God freed us from these terrible assaults and trials.

Martin Luther

* Mt 17:5.   † Jn 14:6.   ‡ Jn 14:9.

Purification of the soul

'The flowers appear on the earth, and the time for pruning is come' (Canticles 2:12). The flowers of the heart are good desires. As soon as they appear we must prune away from our conscience all dead and superfluous works.

The soul seeking to be a bride of Christ must put off the old self and be clothed with the new self, pruning away everything which comes between it and the love of God. This purging is the foundation of our future health.

Ordinary purification and healing of body or soul is accomplished little by little, slowly and patiently. The soul rising from sin to holiness is like the dawn, which as it rises does not at once dispel darkness, but advances gradually. It is an old saying that a slow cure is a certain cure. The spiritual diseases, like those of the body, come quickly and mounted. They go away on foot and slowly. We must be patient and full of courage.

The discipline of purification only ends with life itself. Do not be discouraged by weaknesses; our perfection consists in struggling against them, which we cannot do unless we see them. Nor can we conquer them unless we face up to them. Victory does not lie in ignoring our weaknesses, but in resisting them.

Francis de Sales

Be thou my vision

Be thou my vision, beloved Lord: none other is aught but the King of the seven heavens.

Be thou my meditation by day and night: may it be thou that I behold for ever in my sleep.

Be thou my speech: be thou my understanding: be thou for me: may I be for thee.

Be thou my father: may I be thy son: mayst thou be mine: may I be thine.

Be thou alone my special love: let there be none other save the High-King of heaven.

Thy love in my soul and in my heart – grant this to me, O King of the seven heavens.

Beloved Christ, what'er befall me, O Ruler of all, be thou my vision.

The Celtic Tradition

Over-eagerness a stumbling-block

Why is it that in spite of your attraction to give yourself entirely to God, and your pious reading, you seem to remain always at the entrance of the interior life without the power of entering? I will tell you the reason, my dear sister, for I see it very distinctly; it is because you have misused this attraction by inordinate desires, by over-eagerness, and a natural activity, thus displeasing God, and stifling the gentle action of grace.

Also, because in your conduct there has been a secret and imperceptible presumption which has made you rely on your own industry and your own efforts. Without noticing it you have acted as if you aspired to do all the work by your own industry, and even to do more than God desired.

You who would have taken yourself to task for any worldly ambition, have, without scruple, allowed yourself to be carried away by a still more subtle ambition, and by a desire for a high position in the spiritual life. But, be comforted; thanks to the merciful sternness of God's dealings with you, so far nothing is lost; on the contrary, you have gained greatly. God punishes you for these imperfections like a good father, with tenderness; and enables you to find a remedy for the evil in the chastisement he awards you.

Jean-Pierre de Caussade

Be content to wait on God's action

Abandonment to God is for you just now the one thing necessary. When you go to prayer you must be resigned to suffer exactly as God pleases.

When distractions, aridity, temptations and weariness overwhelm you, say: 'You are welcome, cross of my God; I embrace you with a resigned will; make me suffer until my self-love becomes crucified and dead.' Then remain in God's presence like a beast of burden weighed down by its load and almost ready to perish, but expecting succour and help from its master.

If you could but throw yourself in spirit at the foot of the cross of Jesus Christ, humbly kiss his sacred wounds, and remain there at his divine feet, steadfast and motionless, and do nothing else but wait patiently in silence and peace as a poor beggar waits for hours at a time at the gates of a great king, hoping to receive an alms!

But, before all things, do not dream of making any more efforts, either in prayer or in anything else, trying to be more recollected than God wishes you to be. Be satisfied to know that this state of dissipation displeases you, and that you have a great desire to be recollected; but only when it pleases God, and as much as it pleases him, neither more nor less.

Jean-Pierre de Caussade

No man a stranger

It is clearly true that in this work the second and lower part of charity, that of loving one's fellow-Christian, is truly and perfectly fulfilled.

The reason is that the perfect worker has no special regard for any particular person whether relative or stranger, friend or foe.

He thinks of men alike as his kinsmen and none as strangers. He sees all as friends and none as enemies.

So much is this so, that he regards all who hurt and maltreat him in this life as his best and special friends; and he believes that he is moved to will them as much good as to his most intimate friend.

All will be loved genuinely and sincerely for God; as too will he love himself.

He who would be a perfect disciple of our Lord must ardently lift up his spirit in this spiritual work on behalf of all mankind, as did our Lord in his body on the cross.

Author of 'The Cloud of Unknowing'

A beam of spiritual light

Work hard then, and beat upon this high cloud of unknowing; afterwards you may rest. Anyone who takes on this work unless he be given special grace, or has been long accustomed to it, will find it hard indeed.

The demanding nature of this work is to be found in the putting down of the memory of creatures and in holding them under the cloud of forgetting. This is man's work with the help of grace. The stirring of love, that is God's work. So press on and do your part, and I promise that he will not fail in his.

Work away then. Work hard for a while and the burden will soon be lightened. For although it is hard in the beginning when you lack devotion, after a while when devotion is kindled it will become restful and light.

God will sometimes work all by himself, though not for long at a time and only when and how he wills. You will then be happily content to let him work alone.

It may be that sometimes he will send out a beam of spiritual light piercing the cloud of unknowing that is between you and him, showing you some of his secrets, of which man may not and cannot speak.

Author of 'The Cloud of Unknowing'

Nothing is in vain to the humble soul

Nothing is in vain or without profit to the humble soul; like the bee it takes its honey even from bitter herbs. It stands always in a state of divine growth, and everything that falls upon it is like the dew of heaven to it.

Shut up yourself therefore in this form of humility, all good is enclosed in it; it is a water of heaven that turns the fire of the fallen soul into the meekness of the divine life. Let it be as a garment wherewith you are always covered, and the girdle with which you are girt.

Breathe nothing but in and from its spirit; see nothing but with its eyes; hear nothing but with its ears. And then, whether you are in the church or out of the church, hearing the praises of God or receiving wrongs from men and the world, everything will help forward your growth in the life of God.

William Law

Heaven is within

You know that God is everywhere, which is a great truth; wherever God dwells there is heaven, and you may feel sure that all which is glorious is near His Majesty.

Remember what St Augustine tells us – I think it comes in his Meditations; how he sought God in many places and at last found the Almighty within himself. Do you consider it of slight importance for a soul given to wandering thoughts to realize this truth and to see that it has no need to go to heaven in order to speak to the eternal Father or to enjoy his company? Nor is it requisite to raise the voice to address him, for he hears every whisper however low.

We are not forced to take wings to find him, but have only to seek solitude and to look within ourselves.

Address him sometimes as Father, or as Brother, or again as a Master or as your Bridegroom: sometimes in one way, sometimes in another, he will teach you what he wishes you to do.

Teresa of Avila

A most dangerous temptation

At the moment you are suffering from one of the most dangerous temptations that could assail any soul of goodwill: the temptation to discouragement. I conjure you to resist it with all your might.

Have confidence in God, and be convinced he will finish the work he has begun in you.

Your foolish fears about the future come from the devil. Think only of the present, abandon the future to Providence. It is the good use of the present that assures the future.

Apply yourself to obtaining attachment and conformity to the will of God in all things, and everywhere, even to the smallest things, for in this consists all virtue and perfection.

For the rest, God only allows our daily faults to keep us humble. If you know how to gain this fruit and to remain in peace and confidence, then you will be in a better state than if you had not committed any apparent fault, which would only have greatly flattered your self-love.

Ought we not to admire and bless the infinite goodness of God who knows how to make our very faults serve for our greater good?

Jean-Pierre de Caussade

God carries the soul

Wait upon God with loving
and pure attentiveness,
working no violence on
yourself lest you disturb the
soul's peace and tranquillity.
God will feed your soul
with heavenly food since you
put no obstacle in his way.

The soul in this state must
remember that if it is not conscious of making
progress, it is making much more than when it was
walking on foot, because God himself is bearing it
in his arms. Although outwardly it is doing nothing,
it is in reality doing more than if it were working,
since God is doing the work within it. And it is not
remarkable that the soul does not see this, for our
senses cannot perceive that which God works in the
soul.

Let the soul then leave itself in the hands of God and
have confidence in him. Let it not trust itself to the
hands and works of others, for if it stays in God's
care it will certainly make progress.

John of the Cross

On the necessity of prayer

Prayer brings the mind into the brightness of the divine light and the will to the warmth of divine love. Nothing else so purges the mind of ignorance and the will of wrong inclinations. It is a fountain which revives our good desires and causes them to bring forth fruit; it washes away the stains of our weaknesses and calms the passions of the heart.

Above all, I would recommend mental prayer, the prayer of the heart; and that drawn from the contemplation of the life and Passion of our Lord. If you habitually meditate on him, your soul will be filled with him, you will learn his expression and learn to frame your actions after his example.

He is the light of the world. It is therefore in him, by him and for him that we must be enlightened and illuminated. And so, if we remain close to our Lord, meditating on him and giving heed to his words, we shall gradually by the help of his grace learn to speak, to act and to will like him.

There we must stay, for we can approach God the Father by no other door.

Francis de Sales

The motive is love

[Brother Lawrence wrote]:

I have received today two books and a letter from Sister ——, who is preparing to make her profession, and upon that account desires the prayers of your holy community, and yours in particular . . . I will send you one of these books which treat of the presence of God, a subject which, in my opinion, contains the whole spiritual life: and it seems to me that whoever duly practises it will soon become spiritual.

I know that for the right practice of it the heart must be empty of all else, because God wills to possess the heart alone; and as he cannot possess it alone unless it be empty of all besides, so he cannot work in it what he would unless it be left vacant to him.

There is not in the world a kind of life more sweet and delightful than that of a continual walk with God.

Those only can comprehend it who practise and experience it; yet I do not advise you to do it from that motive.

It is not pleasure which we ought to seek in this exercise; but let us do it from the motive of love, and because God would have us so walk.

Brother Lawrence

We are not blamed

And in this mortal life, mercy and forgiveness are the pathway that always leads to grace. And because of the storms and sorrows that befall us we often seem dead, as many judge on earth. But in God's sight the soul that shall be saved is never dead, and never shall be.

But at this I wondered and was amazed with all the strength of my soul and thought this: 'Good Lord, I see that you are truth itself, and I know truly that we sin grievously all the day long and are much to blame. And I can neither forsake knowing this truth, nor do I see you put any blame on us. How can this be?'

For I know by the daily teaching of Holy Church, and by my own feelings, that the blame for our sin hangs heavy upon us, from the first man until the time we come up to heaven.

This, then, was my wonder – that I saw our Lord putting no more blame upon us than if we were as clean and as holy as the angels in heaven.

Julian of Norwich

Believe and then you will know

We believe, not because we know but so that we may come to know. For what we shall know no eye has seen, no ear heard, nor has man's heart imagined. Faith is to believe what we do not yet see: truth to see what we have believed. To follow after God is to long for happiness, to reach him is that happiness itself.

If we have reached the pathway of faith let us keep to it unswervingly, so that our hearts may become able to know what we do not now understand.

Bring the light of reason to bear on what you now believe firmly by faith.

Could God hate in us that by which he has distinguished us from the beasts? Of course not: we could not in any case believe, if we had not reasonable souls.

There are some things belonging to our salvation which we as yet cannot understand, though one day we shall. In these matters faith should go ahead of reason, purifying the heart and making it able to receive the great light of reason.

The prophet said, unless you believe you shall not understand; thus we may see that it is reasonable for faith to go before. If we are persuaded of this, it is by the small amount of reason which goes before faith.

Augustine

Love shared in heaven

It is God's will here below that we shall distribute to one another by prayer the treasures with which he has enriched us. This is in order that, when we reach our everlasting home, we may love one another with grateful hearts and with affection far beyond that which is present in the most perfect family circle on earth.

In heaven, there will be no looks of indifference, because all the saints owe so much to one another. No envious glances will be cast, because the happiness of each is the happiness of all.

With the doctors of the Church we shall be like doctors; with the martyrs like martyrs, with the virgins like virgins. Just as the members of one family are proud of each other, so without the least jealousy we shall take pride in our heavenly brothers and sisters.

When we see the glory of the great saints, and know that through the secret workings of Providence we have helped them to attain it, our joy and happiness will perhaps be as intense as theirs. A shepherd boy may be the familiar friend of an apostle or a doctor of the Church; a little child may be in close intimacy with a patriarch . . . How I long to enter the kingdom of love!

Thérèse of Lisieux

A journey

I asked the Lord if I should go on a journey; he said, 'Go in my name. I will go with you and bring you back in safety.'

The Lord sent storms so fierce that we expected to be shipwrecked and commended ourselves and our ship to the care of the Lord.

Lord, I came on this journey for love of you and you have promised that I shall be safe. Remember your promises and show me that it was you who directed me to come and not some evil spirit who has led me astray.

The Lord answered me, 'Why are you afraid? Why do you not trust me? I am as powerful on the sea as on the land.'

'I will keep my promises to you. Wait patiently and trust me. Do not waver in your faith, for without faith you grieve me. If you trust and do not doubt, you will gain peace of mind and strength to comfort those with you who are in fear and sorrow.'

Margery Kempe

On preparing to meditate

You may not understand how to practise mental prayer. I will instruct you shortly and simply.

Place yourself in the presence of God by these four means. First, keenly and attentively realize that God is everywhere; there is no place or thing in the world where he is not. Let us go where we will, be where we will, we shall always be where God is.

We do not see God, and although faith tells us that he is present, not seeing him with our own eyes we soon forget, and act as though he were far away. Though as an act of reason we know his presence everywhere, if we do not think about it, the result is the same as if we did not know it.

Secondly, God is specially in your heart and spirit. He is heart of your heart, spirit of your spirit. David calls him the God of his heart (Psalm 17:28).

Thirdly, reflect that our Lord in his humanity looks down always upon us from heaven.

Fourthly, in imagination behold Jesus in his humanity as actually present with us.

Make use of some of these methods to place yourself in God's presence. Let what you do be short and simple.

Francis de Sales

The humble man

No one ever hates, or wounds with words, or despises the person who is humble; and because his Lord loves him he is dear to all. Everyone loves him, everyone cherishes him, and wherever he approaches, people look on him as an angel of light and accord honour to him.

A wise and learned man may speak, but they silence him in order to give the humble an opportunity to speak: the eyes of everyone are fixed on his lips, to see what utterance will issue forth from him. Everyone waits on his words as if they were words from God.

The humble man approaches wild animals, and the moment they catch sight of him their ferocity is tamed. They come up and cling to him as to their Master, wagging their tails and licking his hands and feet. They scent as coming from him the same fragrance that came from Adam before the transgression, the time when they were gathered together before him and he gave them names in Paradise. This scent was taken away from us, but Christ has renewed it and given it back to us at his coming. It is this which has sweetened the fragrance of humanity.

Even the demons with their malice and fierceness, with all the pride of their minds, become like dust once they have encountered a humble person.

Isaac of Syria

Three medicines of the soul

Our Lord holds us tenderly when it seems to us that we are nearly forsaken and cast away because of our sin – and that we deserve to be. And because we are made humble by this we are raised high in God's sight, by his grace, and also by great repentance and compassion and true yearning for God. Then sinners are suddenly delivered from sins and from pain and are taken up to heaven and even made high saints.

Repentance makes us clean; compassion makes us ready; and yearning for God makes us worthy.

These are three ways, as I see it, by which all souls come to heaven – that is to say, those who have been sinners on earth and shall be saved. For by these medicines every soul must be healed.

Julian of Norwich

Shame shall be turned to honour

Though the soul is healed, God still sees the wounds, and sees them not as scars but as honours. And so, by contrast, as we have been punished here with sorrow and penance, we shall be rewarded in heaven with the courteous love of our Lord God almighty. It is his will that no one who comes there shall lose a whit of his labour, for he looks on sin as sorrow and anguish to those who love him and, because he loves them, does not blame them for it.

The reward we receive shall not be small, but it shall be high, glorious and full of praise; and so shame shall be turned to honour and increase of joy. For our courteous Lord does not want his servants to fall into despair even when we fall deeply into sin, for our falling does not stop him loving us.

Peace and love are always alive in us, but we are not always alive to peace and love. But he wills that we understand this: that he is the ground of our whole life in love, and that he is our everlasting protector and mightily defends us against our enemies who fight so hard and fiercely against us. And we need his help all the more because we give them an advantage by our failures.

Julian of Norwich

Different forms of prayer

Every man that has any feeling of the weight of his sin, or any true desire to be delivered from it by Christ has learning and capacity enough to make his own prayer. For praying is not speaking forth eloquently, but simply, the true desire of the heart.

The most simple souls that have accustomed themselves to speak their own desires and wants to God, in such short but true breathings of their hearts to him, will soon know more of prayer and the mysteries of it than any persons who have only their knowledge from learning and learned books.

It is not silence, or a simple petition, or a great variety of outward expressions that alters the nature of prayer, or makes it good or better, but only and solely the reality, steadiness and continuity of the desire; and therefore whether a man offers this desire to God in the silent longing of the heart, or in simple short petitions, or in a great variety of words is of no consequence. But if you would know what I would call a true and great gift of prayer, and what I most of all wish for myself, it is a good heart that stands continually inclined towards God.

William Law

Suffering in peace

To preserve our spirituality
there is no other way apart
from silent suffering and
labour, remaining faithful
to the practice of solitude,
and forgetfulness of all
creatures and outward events
even though the world should
disintegrate about us.

Never fail to keep your heart at peace and in tender
love, ready to suffer as things present themselves.

It is impossible to make progress except by working
and suffering courageously, always in silence.

To have God in everything a soul must have nothing
in everything, for how can a heart belong in any way
to two people at once?

When anything disagreeable happens to you,
remember Christ crucified and keep silent.

John of the Cross

Inward and outward silence

Keep yourself carefully from setting your thoughts upon what happens in the community, and still more from speaking of it except to the proper person and at the proper time. Nor should you ever be shocked or marvel at what you see or hear, but should try to keep your soul forgetful of it all.

For if you want to ponder on all that happens you would always discover something amiss even if you lived among angels.

Strive to keep your soul limpid and pure before God, undisturbed by thoughts of one thing or another.

Keep in mind what the apostle St James says: 'If any man thinks himself to be religious and does not control his tongue, that man's religion is useless.' This is to be understood of inward as well as outward chatter.

John of the Cross

Bereavement

I have been urged by friends of yours to write to you. Please receive this letter kindly. They tell me that since the death of your dear wife, who departed this life at peace with God, you have been trying to help the repose of her soul with good works and services.

First, I beg to remind you of what Job says: 'The Lord gave, and the Lord has taken away; as it seemed good to the Lord, so has he done.'* You should sing the same song to God, a loving and faithful God who gave you a loving and faithful wife, and has now taken her away. She was his before he gave her; she was his after he had given her; and she still remains his (as we all do), even now that he has taken her away.

Although it hurts us when he takes his own from us, his goodwill should be a greater comfort to us than all his gifts, for God is immeasurably more than all his gifts. Although we cannot perceive God's will as clearly as we can see a wife, yet we can perceive and apprehend his will by faith.

Cheerfully give back to God what is his, and accept this proper exchange, this strange barter whereby, instead of a dear, kindly wife, you have a dear, kindly will of God. Nay, more! God himself. Truly, God's goodness and mercy extend beyond this life.

Martin Luther

* Jb 1:21.

On silence

Love silence above everything else, for it brings you near to fruit which the tongue is too feeble to expound.

First of all we force ourselves to be silent, but then from out of our silence something else is born that draws us into silence itself.

May God grant you to perceive that which is born of silence! If you begin in this discipline I do not doubt how much light will dawn in you from it.

After a time a certain delight is born in the heart as a result of the practice of this labour, and it forcibly draws the body on to persevere in stillness.

A multitude of tears is born in us by this discipline, at the wondrous vision of certain things which the heart perceives distinctly, sometimes with pain, and sometimes with wonder.

For the heart becomes small and becomes like a tiny babe: as soon as it clings to prayer, tears burst forth.

Isaac of Syria

The hermit's life

All alone in my little hut without any human being in my company, dear has been the pilgrimage before going to meet death.

Making holy the body with good habits, treading it boldly down: feeble tearful eyes for forgiveness of my passions.

Stepping along the paths of the gospel, singing psalms every hour: an end of talking and long stories: constant bending of the knee.

My Creator to frequent me, my Lord, my King, my spirit to seek him in the eternal kingdom where he is.

All alone in my little hut, all alone so, alone I came into the world, alone I shall go from it.

The Celtic Tradition

Avoid scruples

Perhaps you will ask me how you are to regulate yourself wisely in food and sleep and other such matters. My answer is short: Accept what is offered!

Exercise yourself always without discretion in the work I have set before you, and you will know well enough how to manage properly in other things. I cannot believe that a soul constantly practised in this interior work will err in any of these everyday matters. And if it does, I am bound to think it will always get things wrong.

If I am seriously engaged in this spiritual work within, matters such as eating and drinking, sleeping and speaking will be regarded with an air of indifference. I would prefer to handle them in this way – and so learn discretion – than by a fussy concern which, as it were, kept score of my successes and failures. Believe me, I could never work like that.

So lift up your heart with a blind stirring of love. Use now the word 'sin' and now 'God'. God you would have, and sin you would be without. God you lack, and sin you will. May the good God help you! How greatly you need him!

Author of 'The Cloud of Unknowing'

The Pharisee

Shall a Christian go and live apart from the world, so that he may not be tried by false brethren? Shall he who has progressed in a righteous life separate himself from the rest so that he need not suffer from anyone? Perhaps people suffered from him before he was converted. Has no one anything to put up with from you? It would surprise me – but if it is so, then you are stronger and thus able to endure other people's failings.

Do you propose to shut out bad men from good men's company? If that is what you say, see if you can shut out all evil thoughts from your own heart. Every day we fight with our own heart.

You say you will go apart with a few good men and admit no wicked brother to your society. How do you recognize the man you wish to exclude? Do all come to you with their hearts bare? Those who wish to come do not know themselves, they cannot be proved unless they are tried.

Nowhere in this life are we secure, except in God's promise – only when we have attained to it, when the gates of Jerusalem are shut behind us, shall we be perfectly safe.

Beloved, mark the apostle's words: 'Support one another in charity.'

Augustine

With the Lord as Friend

With so good a Friend and
Captain ever present, himself
the first to suffer, everything
can be borne.

He helps, he strengthens, he
never fails, he is the true
Friend.

I see clearly, and since then have always seen, that if
we are to please God, and if he is to give us his great
graces, everything must pass through the hands of
his most sacred humanity, in whom His Majesty said
that he is well pleased.

I know this by repeated experience: I have seen
clearly that this is the door by which we are to enter,
if we would have his supreme Majesty reveal to us
his great secrets.

Teresa of Avila

Body and soul permeated by this work

Every man or woman who practises this work will find that it so suffuses body and soul, as to make them gracious and attractive to everyone who sees them.

Indeed, if the least attractive man or woman were drawn by grace to work in this way, their appearance would be quickly changed to one of such graciousness, that all good people who saw them would be glad and happy to have them in their company, and would know that in God's grace they were cheered and strengthened by their presence.

Therefore get this gift – all who by grace may do so. Whoever truly has it will know how to rule himself and all that is his.

He will be wise and perceptive in discerning the character of others. It enables him to be at ease with all who would speak to him – 'saints' and 'sinners' alike – without being drawn into sin himself; and all this to the astonishment of those who see him, and at the same time drawing them through grace to the work in which he is being formed.

Author of 'The Cloud of Unknowing'

Our varying capacities for this work

There are some who regard this task as so formidable and daunting that they think that it cannot be achieved without much hard and persevering preliminary work. Even then, they would say, they experience it but rarely and then only in moments of ecstasy.

I would answer such men as humbly as I can by saying that it all rests entirely on the decree and good pleasure of God, who gives every man the grace of contemplation and spiritual working according to his capacity to receive it.

There are some who will not achieve it without long and arduous spiritual labour. It will be but seldom, and then only by virtue of God's special calling, that they will experience the perfection of this work.

On the other hand there are others so attuned in grace and spirit, and so at home with God in this grace of contemplation, that they may have it when they please in the ordinary occupations of life as in sitting, walking, standing or kneeling. And, yet, during this time they have full control of their faculties and may exercise them if they wish; not, it is true, without some difficulty, but without great difficulty.

Author of 'The Cloud of Unknowing'

This way is not for all

If you think that you are physically or spiritually temperamentally unsuited to this work, you may leave it for some other way. Under good direction there will be no danger and you are not to feel guilty about it. In that case I ask you to excuse me. As far as my limited knowledge allows, I have only wanted to help you.

However, read over what I have written two or three times; the more often the better, and the more you will understand. It may well be that some sentence which presented difficulties at the first or second reading will later become clear.

If a man is truly disposed to this work I think it must be that in the reading or speaking of it, or in hearing it read or spoken, he will feel a positive drawing to what it is doing for him. If then you think it is doing you good, thank God with all your heart and in your love for God pray for me.

If there is anything I have written which you would like clarified or developed, let me know together with your own views. I will endeavour to explain it as best I can.

Author of 'The Cloud of Unknowing'

On dryness in prayer

If you find no pleasure or consolation in meditation, do not be disheartened. Sometimes try vocal prayer, confessing your unworthiness and saying with Jacob, 'I will not let you go unless you bless me.'

Or take a book and read attentively until your mind is quickened and reassured. We must pray purely and simply to do homage to God and to show our faithfulness. If God pleases to speak with us and give inward consolation, it is an honour and delight. But if he appears not to notice us, we must not give up, but remain devoutly and meekly in his presence.

He will surely accept our patience and perseverance, and reward us with his consolations. But if not, let us rest contented, remembering we are unworthy even of the honour of standing before him in his presence.

Francis de Sales

We grow into deeper freedom

At the beginning of a new life one's conduct may seem constrained and uneasy because neither the person who is changed, nor others, are accustomed to an altered way of acting. In all things ease comes with practice.

How can a soul which is entirely employed in keeping recollected, in fighting against itself, in compelling itself to do violence in a hundred different ways, both interior and exterior, be expected to appear merry, free, happy, agreeable and amusing? Truly, if I saw it like this, I should have strong doubts of any interior change whatever.

However, are there not some people, you ask, who have a deep interior life, and at the same time appear very gracious outwardly? This is when a sufficiently long experience has made the exercise of interior recollection, in a sort of way, natural to them.

But when they began they were just like you, my dear sister, and the same things that are said of you were said of them. They went their way without taking any notice of what others said, and God at last placed them in a state that is called the liberty of the children of God.

Jean-Pierre de Caussade

Advice on disregarding spiritual sweetness

If a man is moved to love God apart from any sweetness he feels, he is already focusing his love upon God, whom he does not feel.

If he sets his will upon pleasurable and consoling feelings, thinking about them and resting in them, he is setting his will on creatures or related things, making them into an end instead of a means.

That man would be very ignorant who thinks that because sweetness and delight are failing him, God is failing him, or should think that in having these he is having God.

He would be still more ignorant if he followed God looking for sweetness, and rejoiced and rested in it when obtained. In this case his love is not set purely on God alone above all things, for in clinging to and desiring what is created, his will cannot soar to God.

John of the Cross

Treasure-hunting

Let the Lord your God be your hope – seek for nothing else from him, but let him himself be your hope. There are people who hope from him riches or perishable and transitory honours, in short they hope to get from God things which are not God himself. Seek for him alone, and despising everything else, make your way to him. Forget other things, remember him; leave other things behind, stretch out to him. Let him be your hope, who is guiding you to your destination.

Where in the end does coveting this world's goods lead you? You want a farm, then an estate, then you shut your neighbours out and covet their possessions. You extend your desires till you reach the shore. Having made the earth your own, perhaps you want heaven, too?

Leave all your desires. He who made heaven and earth is more beautiful than all; he who made all things is better than all; he will be to you everything you love. Learn to love the Creator in the creature, in the work him who made it. Don't let what was made take such a hold of you that you lose him by whom you yourself were made.

Augustine

Love covers the multitude of sins

It may be that at some future day my present state will appear to me full of defects, but nothing now surprises me. Nor does my utter helplessness distress me. I even glory in it, and expect each day to reveal some fresh imperfection. Indeed, these lights on my own nothingness do me more good than lights on matters of faith.

Remembering that 'Love covers the multitude of sins' (Proverbs 10:12), I draw from the rich mine which Jesus has opened up for us in the Gospels. I search the depth of his words and cry out with the Psalmist: 'I have run in the way of your commandments since you have enlarged my heart' (Psalm 119:32).

Only love can enlarge my heart. Jesus, ever since the flame of love consumes me, I run with delight in the way of your new commandment, and I desire to run until that glorious day when I follow you to your Kingdom, singing the canticle of love.

God in his goodness has given me a clear insight into the deep mysteries of love. If only I could express what I know, you would hear heavenly music; but I can only stammer like a child, and if the words of Jesus were not my support, I would be tempted to hold my peace.

Thérèse of Lisieux

The way of the returning prodigal

Jacob Behmen★ absolutely requires his reader to be in the way of the returning prodigal. It is not rules of morality observed, or an outward blameless form of life that will do: for pride, vanity, envy, self-love and love of the world can be and often are the heart of such a morality of life. But the state of the lost son is quite another thing.

As soon as he comes to himself and has seeing eyes, he will then, like him, see himself far from home; that he has lost his first paradise, his heavenly Father, and the dignity of his first birth; that he is a poor, beggarly slave in a foreign land, hungry, ragged, and starving among the lowest kind of beasts, not so well fed and clothed as they are.

Wherever the gospel itself is received and professed without something of this preparation of heart, without this sensibility of the lost son, there it can only be a stone of stumbling and help the earthly man to form a religion of notions and opinions from the unfelt meaning of the letter of the gospel.

William Law

★ Jacob Boehme was so called by Law and his contemporaries.

The peril of disunity

Beware of schism, of making a rent in the Church of Christ. That inward disunion, the members ceasing to have a reciprocal love 'one for another', is the very root of all contention and every outward separation. Beware of everything tending thereto. Beware of a dividing spirit: shun whatever has the least aspect that way.

Suffer not one thought of separating from your brethren, whether their opinion agrees with yours or not. Do not dream that any man sins in not believing you, in not taking your word; or that this or that opinion is essential to the work, and both must stand or fall together.

Beware of impatience with contradiction. Do not condemn or think hardly of those who cannot see just as you see, or who judge it their duty to contradict you, whether in a great thing or a small. I fear some of us have thought hardly of others merely because they contradicted what we affirmed. All this tends to division; and by everything of this kind, we are teaching them an evil lesson against ourselves.

O beware of touchiness, of testiness, not bearing to be spoken to; starting at the least word; and flying from those who do not implicitly receive mine or another's sayings!

John Wesley

On ejaculatory prayers

We make our recollection in God because we long for him, and we long for him so that we may be recollected – so the one helps the other, and both arise from holy thoughts. You should therefore seek after God by short but ardent efforts of your heart.

Wonder at his beauty, invoke his aid, cast yourself in spirit at the foot of the cross, adore his goodness, speak frequently to him about your salvation; hold out your hand to him as a child to his father, that he may guide you. In every way excite your heart to the love of God.

This prayer is not difficult to practise. It can be interwoven with all our business and occupations without hindering them in the slightest degree. Indeed, our external pursuits are helped rather than hindered by our recollection and short ejaculations from the heart.

There are many useful collections of short vocal prayers, but I advise you not to confine yourself to any formal words. It is better to use those which are prompted by the feelings of your heart, as you need them. They will never fail you. But some surpass others, like the various invocations of the name of Jesus.

Francis de Sales

The Church

In the communion of saints we are all brothers and sisters so closely united that a closer relationship cannot be conceived. For in this fellowship we have one baptism, one Christ, one sacrament, one food, one gospel, one faith, one Spirit, one spiritual body; and each is a member one of another. No other society is so deeply rooted, so closely knit. For, while natural brothers possess one flesh, one heritage, one home, nevertheless, eventually they must part from one another and merge with another heritage and another blood in marriage.

We are all one with the holy fathers and prophets of the Old Testament; they looked for the promise and believed in it; we see it and believe in it.

The people of God, in other words, the Church, are simply those who rely on nothing else but God's grace and mercy.

God cannot, and God will not allow anybody but himself to rule the soul of man.

Martin Luther

Uneasiness, foolish fears and depression

I can find no particular sin in your conduct, yet I perceive defects and imperfections which might do you great harm if you did not apply a strong remedy. These are uneasiness, foolish fears, depression, weariness, and a discouragement not quite free from deliberation, or at least not combated with sufficient energy, all of which tend to diminish interior peace.

'But what can I do to prevent them?' This: Never retain them wilfully; never parley with them, nor yet combat them with effort, nor violence, which would make them doubly hurtful. Drop them as one drops a stone into the water, think of something else, speak to God of other things, then take refuge in the interior silence of respect, submission, confidence and a total abandonment.

'But', you say, 'supposing that in these or in other matters I commit faults, how ought I to behave?' Well! then you must bear in mind the advice of St Francis de Sales: do not trouble yourself about your troubles, do not be uneasy about your uneasiness, do not be discouraged because you are discouraged, but return immediately to God without violence, even thanking him for having prevented you from falling into greater faults.

Jean-Pierre de Caussade

A poultice to your sick self

Take good, gracious God as he is, and lay him as a poultice on your sick self as you are. Or, if I may put it otherwise, begin with your disordered self and, just as you are, reach out in desire to touch good, gracious God as he is.

Do we not know from the Gospels that simply to touch God is endless health? 'If I but touch the hem of his garment I shall be healed': so said the woman who came to him. Much more then shall you be healed of the sickness of your soul by this lovely heavenly touching of God himself.

Step out then resolutely and apply this sovereign remedy. Just as you are, lift up your sick self to God as he is – our God is good and gracious.

Do this without introspection concerning yourself, without speculation concerning God. Forget all about concepts like clean or unclean, spiritual or material, divine or human. All that now matters is that, stripped of all conceptual thought, you contemplate God in the eager longing of love. So shall you be graciously united in spirit to the lovely being of God himself – God as he is – that and no more.

Author of 'The Cloud of Unknowing'

Wisdom and folly

I have understood two opposites – one is the wisest thing that anyone may do in this life, the other is the most foolish. The wisest thing is for a person to act according to the will and counsel of his greatest friend. This blessed friend is Jesus. It is his will and counsel that we should stay with him, and hold ourselves closely to him for ever, in whatever state we may be; for whether we are clean or foul it is all one to his love.

Through good and ill, he wills that we never turn from him. But because of the contradictions in us, we often fall into sin.

And then we are made fearful by our enemy and through our own folly and blindness, which say to us, 'You know well that you are a wretch, a sinner and faithless. You do not keep the commandments. You are always promising our Lord you will do better, and, starting right away, you fall into the same sin – especially sloth and wasting time.' For this is the beginning of sin in my sight, particularly for those who have given themselves to serve God by holding his blessed goodness in their hearts.

Julian of Norwich

The strength of humility

He says, 'Do not blame yourself too much, thinking that your trouble and distress is all your fault. For it is not my will that you should be unduly sad and despondent.'

Our enemy tries to depress us by false fears which he proposes. His intention is to make us so weary and dejected, that we let the blessed sight of our everlasting friend slip from our minds.

It is a beautiful humility – brought about by the grace and mercy of the Holy Spirit – when a sinful soul willingly and gladly accepts the chastisement our Lord himself would give us. It will seem light and easy, if only we will accept contentedly what he calls upon us to bear.

We must humbly and patiently bear and endure the penance God himself gives us, keeping his blessed Passion in mind. For when we hold his Passion in our minds with pity and love, then we suffer with him, as did his friends that saw it.

Julian of Norwich

Saints

Bright, bright
The fellowship of saints in light,
Far, far beyond all earthly sight.
No plague can blight, no foe destroy.
United here they live in love:
O then, above how deep their joy!

Set free
By Jesu's mortal wounds are we,
Blest with rich gifts – and more shall be.
Blessings has he in endless store:
Some drops are showered upon us here;
What when we hear the ocean's roar?

Deep, deep
The feast of life and peace they keep
In that fair world beyond death's sleep.
Our hearts will leap their joys to see
Who, with the Lamb's dear merits graced,
All sorrow past, reign glad and free.

The Celtic Tradition

Death

At birth a child comes forth amid pain and danger, from the narrow dwelling of the mother's womb, into the broad light of day. In a similar way a man goes through the narrow gate of death when he departs this life. And though heaven and earth under which we now live appear so wide, so vast, yet, in comparison with the heaven that shall be, it is far narrower and much smaller than is the womb in comparison with the broad expanse of heaven. That is why the death of saints is called a new birth, and their festivals birthdays. A woman, when she is in travail, has sorrow, because her hour is come; but as soon as she is delivered of the child, she remembers no more the anguish for joy that a man is born into the world. Likewise in death. We wrestle in anguish, yet know that hereafter we shall come forth into a wide, open space, and into eternal joy.

When I feel the dread of death, I say, 'O death, you have nothing to do with me, because I have another death which kills my death. And the death which kills is stronger than that which is killed.'

God appointed death to be the destroyer of death. It is evidence for God's surpassing goodness, that after death has entered,* it is not permitted to hurt us *ultimately*, but is taken captive at the outset, and made to be the punishment and death of sin.

Martin Luther

* Gn 3:19.

Choosing God in all circumstances

The more God gives the more he makes us desire, until we are empty and he is able to fill us with good things.

The immense benefits of God can only be contained by empty and solitary hearts. Therefore our Lord, who loves you greatly, wishes you to be quite alone, for he desires to be your only companion.

You must needs apply your mind to him alone, and in him alone content yourself, that in him you may find all consolation. Although God is always with us, if we set our hearts on other things beside him we cannot be at peace.

God knows what is best for all, and orders affairs for our good. Think on this only, that all is ordained by God. And pour in love where there is no love, and you will draw love out.

John of the Cross

What have I on earth but thee?

No Christian can say he has no tribulations – why? Because as long as we are in the body, we are only journeying to God. However well off we may be we are not yet in our homeland. A man cannot love the journey and his own country too. If he loves his country, the journey will seem wearisome and full of tribulations. Here, we labour and sorrow: there, is endless rest and unwearied love.

But, you will say, I have all I want. Have you? Are you sure that it won't all disappear? But I'm richer now, I've made a lot of money: possibly you are more afraid than you were, you might have felt more secure when you were poorer. But suppose you have everything, are rich in this world's goods and feel sure of them too, and moreover God says to you: 'All this will go on for ever, you shall possess these things for ever – but you will never see my face.'

Brethen, ask the spirit, not the flesh. Let faith, hope and charity which are beginning to grow in your hearts give your reply. Think: would all those possessions make us happy if we were never to see his face? God forbid that anyone rest his joy in them and seek for nothing more. Such a man has not begun to love God, to live as a pilgrim. Nothing that we have except God can really be sweet to us. He is the giver of all things; without him himself what arc they to us?

Augustine

In time of trouble

When the soul is tempest-tossed, troubled and cut off by worries, then is the time to pray, so as to make the soul willing and responsive towards God. But there is no kind of prayer that can make God more responsive to the soul, for God is always constant in love.

And so I saw that, whenever we feel the need to pray, our good Lord follows us, helping our desire.

And when, by his special grace, we behold him clearly, knowing no other need, then we follow him and he draws us to himself by love.

For I saw and understood that his great overflowing love brings all our gifts to fulfilment.

I saw, too, that his unceasing work in everything is done so well, so wisely and so mightily that it is beyond our power to imagine, or guess, or think.

Julian of Norwich

The one will of love

As love has no by-ends, wills nothing but its own increase, so everything is as oil to its flame; it must have that which it wills, and cannot be disappointed, because everything naturally helps it to live in its own way, and to bring forth its own work.

The spirit of love does not want to be rewarded, honoured or esteemed; its only desire is to propagate itself, and become the blessing and happiness of everything that wants it. And therefore it meets wrath and evil and hatred and opposition with the same one will as the light meets the darkness, only to overcome it with all its blessings.

Did you want to avoid the wrath or ill-will, or to gain the favour of any persons, you might easily miss of your ends; but if you have no will but to all goodness, everything you meet, be it what it will, must be forced to be assistant to you. For the wrath of an enemy, the treachery of a friend, and every other evil only help the spirit of love to be more triumphant, to live its own life and find all its own blessings in a higher degree.

William Law

Our hearts are his Kingdom

Let us realize that we have within us a most splendid palace built entirely of gold and precious stones – in short, one that is fit for such a Lord – and that we are partly responsible for the condition of this building, because there is no structure so beautiful as a soul full of pure virtues, and the more perfect these virtues are, the more brilliantly do the jewels shine.

Within this palace dwells the mighty King who has deigned to become your Father and who is seated on a throne of priceless value, by which I mean your heart.

Had I understood always, as I do now, that so great a King resided in my soul, I should not have left him alone so often, but should have stayed with him sometimes and not have kept his dwelling-place in such disorder.

He does not force our wills but only takes what we give him, but he does not give himself entirely until he sees that we yield ourselves entirely to him.

Teresa of Avila

On continually thinking of God

Those who are filled with an earthly love are always thinking of the object of their attachment, their heart brims with affection for it, their mouth is always full of its praise. When absent, they constantly speak their love in letters, engrave the treasured name on every tree.

In the same way those who love God are never tired of thinking of him, living for him, seeking him and talking to him. They would like to engrave the holy name of Jesus on the heart of every human being in the world.

To such people, everything speaks of God, and all creation joins them in praising the loved one. The whole world speaks to them in a silent but intelligible language of their love, everything excites them to holy thoughts, from which arises a stream of ejaculatory prayers to God.

The habit of recollection and ejaculatory prayers is the keystone of devotion and can supply the defects of all your other prayers, but nothing else can fill its place. Without it, you cannot follow the contemplative life well, or the active life without danger.

Francis de Sales

Dependence on God alone

Let us depend, then, on God alone, for he never changes; he knows better than we do what is necessary for us, and, like a good father, is always ready to give it.

But he has to do with children who are often so blind that they do not see for what they are asking. Even in their prayers, that to them seem so sensible and just, they deceive themselves by desiring to arrange the future which belongs to God alone.

When he takes away from us what we consider necessary, he knows how to supply its place imperceptibly, in a thousand different ways unknown to us.

This is so true that bitterness and heaviness of heart borne with patience and interior silence make the soul advance more than would the presence and instruction of the holiest and most skilful director.

I have had a hundred experiences of this and am convinced that, at present, this is your path, and the only things that God asks of you are submission, abandonment, confidence, sacrifice and silence.

Practise these virtues as well as you can without too violent efforts.

Jean-Pierre de Caussade

The soul must stay with Christ

My soul stays with Christ.

These are very precious, valuable and noteworthy words (John 6:32–35 on the Bread of Life), which we must not only know but turn them to our profit and say, 'With these words I shall go to bed in the evening and arise in the morning; on them I shall rely, on them I shall sleep, wake and work, and with them cross the final bridge of death into eternal life.'

Seek yourself only in Christ and not in yourself; then you will find yourself in him eternally.

The one doctrine which I have supremely at heart is that of faith in Christ, from whom, through whom and unto whom all my theological thinking flows back and forth, day and night.

To preach Christ means to feed the soul, to make it righteous, to set it free and to save it, if it believe the preaching. For faith alone is the saving and efficacious use of the word of God.★

Christ ought to be preached to the end that faith in him be established, that he may not only be Christ, but be Christ for you and for me, and that what is said of him, and what his name denotes, may be effectual in us.

Martin Luther

★ Rm 10:9; 10:4; 1:17; Hab 2:4.

Suffering for Christ's sake

Expect contradiction and opposition, together with crosses of various kinds. Consider the words of St Paul: 'To you it is given, on behalf of Christ' – for his sake, as a fruit of his death and intercession for you – 'not only to believe, but also to suffer for his sake.'

It is given! God gives you this opposition or reproach; it is a fresh token of his love. And will you disown the Giver, or spurn his gift, and count it a misfortune? Will you not rather say, 'Father, the hour is come, that thou shouldst be glorified. Now thou givest thy child to suffer something for thee. Do with me according to thy will.'

Know that these things, far from being hindrances to the work of God, or to your soul, unless by your own fault, are not only unavoidable in the course of providence, but profitable, yea, necessary for you. Therefore receive them from God (not from chance) with willingness, with thankfulness. Receive them from men with humility, meekness, yieldingness, gentleness, sweetness.

John Wesley

On the Eucharist

I have not yet said anything about the most sacred of all devotions – the holy and sacred sacrifice and sacrament of the Eucharist, the heart of the Christian religion. It is an ineffable mystery which embraces the untold depths of divine love, and in which God, giving himself to us, bestows freely upon us all his blessings and graces.

Prayer united to this divine sacrifice has unutterable power. Endeavour if possible to be present each day at holy Mass, so that together with the priest you may offer the sacrifice of your Redeemer to God his Father on your own behalf and that of the whole Church. What a privilege it is to be united in so blessed and mighty an action!

If you are unavoidably prevented from being present at the celebration of this great sacrifice by real and bodily presence, do not fail to join in it by a spiritual communion. So that, if you cannot go to church, at least go there in spirit, unite your intention with all your brethren and offer the same spiritual service that you would offer if you were able to be present in person.

If you wish to make your daily meditation at this time, turn your mind to offering this sacrifice through your prayer and meditation.

Francis de Sales

The natural state of our tempers

The natural state of our tempers has a variety of covers, under which they lie concealed at times, both from ourselves and others; but when this or that accident happens to displace such or such a cover, then that which lay hidden under it breaks forth. And then we vainly think that this or that outward occasion has not shown us how we are within, but has only infused or put into us a wrath, or grief, or envy which is not our natural state, or of our own growth, or has all that it has from our own inward state.

But this is mere blindness and self-deceit, for it is as impossible for the mind to have any grief or wrath or joy but what it has all from its own inward state, as for the instrument to give forth any other harmony or discord but that which is within and from itself.

Persons, things and occurrences may strike our instrument improperly and variously, but as we are in ourselves, such is our outward sound, whatever strikes us. If our inward state is the renewed life of Christ within us, then every thing and occasion, let it be what it will, only makes the same life to sound forth and show itself.

William Law

Doing all for God's sake

[Brother Lawrence said]:

That without being discouraged on account of our sins, we should pray for God's grace with perfect confidence, relying on the infinite merits of our Lord Jesus Christ.

God never failed to offer us his grace at every action; he himself distinctly perceived it, and never failed of it, unless when his thoughts had wandered from a sense of God's presence, or he had forgotten to ask his assistance.

God always gives us light in our doubts when we have no other design but to please him, and to act for his love.

Our sanctification does not depend on our changing our work, but in doing that for God's sake which commonly we do for our own.

It was lamentable to see how many people mistook the means for the end, addicting themselves to certain works, which they performed very imperfectly, by reason of their human or selfish regard.

Brother Lawrence

In penitence we are healed

To be like our Lord perfectly is our true salvation and fullest joy. And if we do not know how this may be, we shall ask our Lord and he will teach us. For it is his joy and his glory. Blessed may he be!

In his mercy our Lord shows us our sin and our weakness by the kindly light of himself. For, our sin is so vile and so horrible that he, in his courtesy, will not show it to us except by the light of his grace and mercy.

He, in his courtesy, limits the amount we see, for it is so vile and so horrible that we could not bear to see it as it is. And so, by humbly knowing our sins through contrition and grace, we shall be broken from all things that are not like our Lord. Then shall our blessed Saviour wholly heal us and make us one with him.

The greatest worship we can give him is, in penitence, to live gladly and gaily because of his love.

Julian of Norwich

God's quickening touch

And when we have fallen, through frailty or blindness, then our courteous Lord touches us, stirs and calls us. And then he wills that we should see our wretchedness and humbly acknowledge it. But it is not his will that we should stay like this, nor does he will that we should busy ourselves too much with self-accusation; nor is it his will that we should despise ourselves. But he wills that we should quickly turn to him.

He is quick to clasp us to himself, for we are his joy and his delight, and he is our salvation and our life.

Wonderful and splendid is the place where the Lord lives. And therefore it is his will that we turn quickly at his gracious touch, rejoicing more in the fullness of his love than sorrowing over our frequent failures.

Julian of Norwich

Prayer in practice in love of one another

So far as you can without offending God, try to be genial and to behave in such a way with those you have to deal with that they may take pleasure in your conversation and may wish to imitate your life and manners, instead of being frightened and deterred from virtue.

The more holy someone is, the more cordial should they be with others.

Although you may be pained because their conversation is not what you would wish, never keep aloof if you want to help them and win their love.

Try to think rightly about God, sisters. He does not look at such trifling matters as you suppose; do not alarm your soul or lose courage for you might lose greatly. Keep a pure intention and a firm resolve not to offend God, as I said, but do not trammel your soul, for instead of advancing in sanctity you would contract a number of imperfections and would not help others as you might have done.

Teresa of Avila

Prayer

In meditation I heard the Lord say, 'Which seems to you the better prayer, to pray to me with your heart or with your thoughts?'

'When you pray with your thoughts you know what you ask me and you understand what I say to you. When you sit still and give your heart to meditation, then you will receive thoughts that God has put into your mind.'

'I accept all your prayers whether you speak them, think in your heart, read, or listen to reading.'

'Fasting, penance and saying the daily offices are good when you are learning to pray, and I accept any form of prayer gladly, but you are much closer to me when you sit quietly in contemplation.'

Margery Kempe

Green wood for the burning

When you throw a very dry piece of wood that will burn easily, on the fire, the flame seizes it at once and consumes it quietly and noiselessly.

But if you throw green wood on the fire, the flame does not affect it except for a moment, and then the heat of the fire acting on the green wet wood makes it exude moisture and emit sighing sounds, and twists and turns it in a hundred different ways with great noise, until it has been made dry enough for the flame to take hold of it.

Then the flame consumes it without effort or noise, but quietly.

This is an image of the action of divine love on souls that are still full of imperfections and the evil inclinations of self-love.

They must be purified, refined and cleared away and this cannot be achieved without trouble and suffering.

Look upon yourself, then, as this green wood acted on by divine love before it is able to enkindle it, and to consume it with its flames.

Jean-Pierre de Caussade

On death

Reveal your presence
And let the vision of your
    beauty kill me.
Behold, the malady
Of love is incurable
Except in your presence and
    before your face.

Death can hold no bitterness
for the soul that loves. It
brings with it all the sweetness and delights of love. There is no sadness in the remembrance of it when it opens the door to all joy. Nor can it be painful and oppressive when it is the end of all unhappiness and sorrow and the beginning of all good. Yes, the soul looks upon it as a friend and bride, and rejoices in thinking of it as the day of espousals. It yearns for the day and hour of death more than earthly kings long for principalities and kingdoms.

True love accepts with perfect resignation, yes, even with joy, whatever comes to it from the hand of the Beloved, for 'perfect love casts out fear'.

John of the Cross

Divine love

Divine love is perfect peace and joy, it is a freedom from all disquiet, it is all content and mere happiness and makes everything to rejoice in itself.

Love is the Christ of God. Wherever it comes, it comes as the blessing and happiness of every natural life, as the restorer of every lost perfection, a redeemer from all evil, a fulfiller of all righteousness, and a peace of God which passeth all understanding.

Through all the universe of things nothing is uneasy, unsatisfied or restless but because it is not governed by love, or because its nature has not reached or attained the full birth of the spirit of love. For when that is done every hunger is satisfied, and all complaining, murmuring, accusing, resenting, revenging and striving are as totally suppressed and overcome as the coldness, thickness and horror of darkness are suppressed and overcome by the breaking-forth of the light.

If you ask why the spirit of love cannot be displeased, cannot be disappointed, cannot complain, accuse, resent or murmur, it is because divine love desires nothing but itself, it is its own good, it has all when it has itself, because nothing is good but itself and its own working; for love is God and he that dwells in God dwells in love.

William Law

Love, the highest gift

Love is the highest gift of God; humble, gentle, patient love. All visions, revelations, manifestations whatever are little things compared to love.

It were well you should be thoroughly sensible of this – the heaven of heavens is love. There is nothing higher in religion; there is, in effect, nothing else. If you look for anything but more love, you are looking wide of the mark, you are getting out of the royal way.

And when you are asking others, 'Have you received this or that blessing?' if you mean anything but more love, you mean wrongly. You are leading them out of the way, and putting them upon a false scent.

Settle it, then, in your heart that from the moment God has saved you from all sin, you are to aim at nothing more but more of that love described in the thirteenth chapter of Corinthians. You can go no higher than this until you are carried into Abraham's bosom.

John Wesley

On patience

Our Lord himself said, 'In patience you shall possess your souls' (Luke 21:19). The great happiness of man is to possess his soul; the more perfect our patience is, the more perfectly we possess our souls.

Remember often that it was by suffering and endurance that our Lord saved us; and it is right that we for our part should work out our salvation through sufferings and afflictions, bearing injuries, contradictions and annoyances with great calm and gentleness.

Do not limit your patience to this or that injury or trouble, but let it embrace every sort of trial that God permits to come upon you.

The patient servant of God bears the troubles that bring contempt no less willingly than those that are esteemed honourable.

Be patient not only under the great and heavy trials which come upon you, but also under the minor troubles and accidents of life.

We must be patient not only under sickness, but must bear the particular complaint which God permits.

Francis de Sales

Patience in trials and sickness

Some, when they are sick, afflicted or aggrieved
avoid complaining or appearing hurt, thinking that
to do so is to show their lack of courage and
generosity. They like others to sympathize and find
ways of encouraging them to do so, but want to
appear brave as well as afflicted. Theirs is a false
patience which is really refined ambition and vanity.

A truly patient person neither complains nor wants
anyone else to complain for him. He speaks honestly
and simply of his trial without moaning or exaggeration. If he is pitied, he receives pity with patience,
unless he is wrongly pitied, when he says so.

When you are sick, offer to Christ all your pains,
your suffering and your listlessness. Ask him to unite
them to those he bore for you. Obey your doctor,
take your medicine, your food and your remedies for
love of God, remembering how he tasted gall
for love of mankind.

Desire to recover in order to serve him, but be
prepared to suffer on in obedience to his will, and
prepare to die when he calls you, that you may be
with him and praise him for ever.

Francis de Sales

The Kingdom of God

'The Kingdom of God', saith our blessed Lord, 'is within you.' It is no outward, no distant thing; but 'a well of living water' in the soul, 'springing up into everlasting life'. It is 'righteousness, and peace, and joy in the Holy Ghost'. It is holiness and happiness.

The general manner in which it pleases God to set it up in the heart is this. A sinner, being drawn by the love of the Father, enlightened by the Son ('the true light who lighteth every man that cometh into the world') and convinced of sin by the Holy Ghost; through the preventing grace which is given him freely, cometh weary and heavy-laden, and casteth all his sins upon him that is 'mighty to save'.

He receiveth from him true, living faith. Being justified by faith, he hath peace with God. He rejoices in hope of the glory of God, and knows that sin has no more dominion over him. And the love of God is shed abroad in his heart, producing all holiness of heart and conversation.

John Wesley

Against zeal

A zealous person never achieves peace of mind. And he who is deprived of peace is deprived of joy.

If, as is said, peace of mind is perfect health, and zeal is opposed to peace, then a person stirred by zeal is ill with a grievous sickness.

While you presume to stir up your zeal against the sickness of others, you will have banished health from your own soul. You should rather concern yourself with your own healing. But if you wish to heal those that are sick, know that the sick have greater need of loving care than of rebukes.

Zeal is not reckoned among mankind as a form of wisdom; rather it is one of the sicknesses of the soul, arising from narrow-mindedness and deep ignorance.

The beginning of divine wisdom is the serenity acquired from generosity of soul and forbearance with human infirmities.

For he says, 'You who are strong should bear the infirmities of the weak',* and 'Put right the transgressor with a humble spirit.'† The Apostle numbers peace and long-suffering among the fruits of the Holy Spirit.

Isaac of Syria

* Rm 15:1.   † Ga 6:1.

Hospitality

A brother came to see a certain hermit and, as he was leaving, he said, 'Forgive me, abba, for preventing you from keeping your rule.' The hermit replied, 'My rule is to welcome you with hospitality and to send you away in peace.'

It was said of an old man that he dwelt in Syria on the way to the desert. This was his work: whenever a monk came from the desert, he gave him refreshment with all his heart. Now one day a hermit came and he offered him refreshment. The other did not want to accept it, saying he was fasting. Filled with sorrow, the old man said to him, 'Do not despise your servant, I beg you, do not despise me, but let us pray together. Look at the tree which is here; we will follow the way of whichever of us causes it to bend when he kneels on the ground and prays.' So the hermit knelt down to pray and nothing happened. Then the hospitable one knelt down and at once the tree bent towards him. Taught by this, they gave thanks to God.

The Desert Fathers

No anger except on man's part

For I saw no anger, except on man's part, and God forgives this anger in us. For anger is no more than a perversity and striving against peace and love.

And it is caused either by lack of strength, or lack of wisdom, or lack of goodness. This lack is not found in God, but in us.

For we, because of sin and earthliness, have an earthly and continuous striving against peace and love. And he showed that he recognized this many times, by the lovely look of compassion and pity in his face.

For the root of mercy is love, and the work of mercy is our safekeeping in love. And this was shown in such a way that I could not see any part of mercy separately but, as it were, all one love.

Mercy is a sweet, gracious working of love, mingled with pity in plenty. For mercy works and keeps us safe – and mercy works and turns all things to good for us.

And when I saw all this, I needs must grant that the purpose of God's mercy and of his forgiveness is to lessen and quench our anger.

Julian of Norwich

The Lord is my judge

Jesus, you never ask what is impossible. You know better than I do how frail and imperfect I am. You know I shall never love others as you have loved them, unless you love them yourself within me. It is because you desire to grant me this grace, that you give a new commandment. I cherish it dearly, since it proves to me that it is your will to love in me all those you tell me to love.

When I show love towards others, I know that it is Jesus who is acting within me. The more closely I am united to him, the more dearly I love others. Should I wish to increase this love, and am put off by the defects of another person, I immediately try to look for that person's virtues and good motives. I call to mind that though I may have seen one fall, many victories over self may have been gained but have been concealed through humility. It can also be that what appears to be a fault may be an act of virtue, since it was prompted by an act of virtue.

I have less difficulty in persuading myself that this is so, because of my own experience. Since my small acts of virtue can be mistaken for imperfections, why should not an imperfection be taken for a virtue? Since the Lord is my judge, I will try always to think leniently of others, that he may judge me leniently – or not at all, since he says 'Judge not and you will not be judged' (Luke 6:37).

Thérèse of Lisieux

Prayer in the Spirit

A person is deemed worthy of constant prayer once he has become a dwelling-place of the Spirit.

For unless someone has received the gift of the Comforter, in all certainty he will not be able to accomplish this constant prayer in quiet.

But once the Spirit dwells in someone, as the Apostle says, the Spirit never ceases but prays continuously: then whether he sleeps or wakes, prayer is never absent from that person's soul.

If he eats or drinks, goes to sleep or is active; yes, even if he is sunk in deep sleep, the sweet fragrance of prayer effortlessly breathes in his heart.

Then he is in the possession of prayer that knows no limit. For at all times, even when he is outwardly still, prayer constantly ministers within him secretly.

The silence of the serene is prayer, as one of those clothed in Christ says, for their thoughts are divine stirrings.

The stirring of a pure mind constitutes still utterances, by means of which such people sing in a hidden way to the hidden God.

Isaac of Syria

Full joy in him

The greatest blessedness is to know God in the clear light of eternal life – seeing him truly, experiencing him tenderly, possessing him completely in the fullness of joy.

I saw that sin is so contrary to blessedness, that so long as we have anything to do with it, we shall never see clearly the blessed face of our Lord.

He will never have full joy in us until we have full joy in him, truly seeing his lovely, blessed face.

I hope that by his grace he will continue to draw our outward appearance more and more into conformity with our inward gladness, making us all one with him and with each other in the true and eternal joy which is Jesus.

Julian of Norwich

In touch with God

Jesus said, 'Nobody on earth can know how you commune with me, even you can hardly understand your feelings for me. It is foolish for people in the world to judge you when only God knows what is in your heart.'

'Sometimes I am hidden in your soul. I withdraw until you feel that you have no goodness in your self and you know that all goodness comes from me. Then you know what pain it is to be without me and the joy it is to feel me with you and it makes you eager to seek me again.'

'You have good reason to rejoice and be happy in your soul; my love for you is so great that I cannot withdraw it.'

'Every good thought you have in your heart is the word of God, even if at times you do not hear me clearly.'

Margery Kempe

The inward strong man of pride

The inward strong man of pride, the diabolical self, has his higher works within; he dwells in the strength of the heart, and has every power and faculty of the soul offering continual incense to him.

His memory, his will, his understanding, his imagination are always at work for him and for no one else. His memory is the faithful repository of all the fine things that self has ever done; and lest anything of them should be lost or forgotten, she is continually setting them before his eyes. His will, though it has all the world before it, yet goes after nothing but as self sends it. His understanding is ever upon the stretch for new projects to enlarge the dominions of self; and if this fails, imagination comes in as the last and truest support of self; she makes him a king and mighty lord of castles in the air.

This is that full-born natural self that must be pulled out of the heart and totally denied, or there can be no disciple of Christ; which is only saying this plain truth, that the apostate, self-idolatrous nature of the old man must be put off, or there can be no new creature in Christ.

William Law

The approaches of dawn

My beloved is the mountains,
The solitary wooded valleys,
The strange islands,
The raging torrents,
The whisper of the amorous
  breezes.

The tranquil night
At the approaches of dawn,
The silent music,
The murmuring solitude,
The supper which revives and enkindles love.

The divine light is here very appropriately called the approaches of dawn, that is, the twilight. For as the twilight of the morn disperses the light of day, so the mind, tranquil and reposing in God, is raised up from the darkness of natural knowledge to the morning light of the supernatural knowledge of God.

The soul says that the Beloved is silent music because in him this harmony of spiritual music is understood and experienced.

As every one of the saints received the gifts of God in a different way, so every one of them sings his praises in a different way, and yet all harmonize in one concert of love.

John of the Cross

Freely, freely you have received

To hope that the eternal God will give you this world's goods or the devil everlasting life is equally monstrous. Keep your eye on the ball, keep to the right road.

If your legs are strong, so much the better – run – the faster you move, the sooner you will get home. But perhaps you limp a bit? All right, only don't leave the way, you will get there even if a little late. Don't stick on the way or turn back, don't wander off.

What are we to make of this? Are only those who have not sinned blessed? No, those are blessed whose sins are forgiven. That grace is given to us freely: we have no good works to show and yet he forgives us our sins.

If you look at your deeds you see wickedness, and if God rewards them you would be damned, for 'the wages of sin is death'. But see, God does not exact the payment for sin, but gives you freely grace which is not owed to you.

Punishment is your due, forgiveness is what you receive, and with this forgiveness your faith begins, and with his love, you will begin to do right. Only don't glory in yourself, or be puffed up. Remember what you were when he found you. Reflect that you are a sinner, and then realize that through faith by love you have begun to do well, and this not of your own strength but by the grace of God.

Augustine

Luther's prayer on his deathbed (1546)

O heavenly Father, God of all comfort, I thank thee that thou hast revealed to me thy beloved Son, Jesus Christ, in whom I have believed, whom I have preached and confessed, whom I have loved and praised . . .

I pray thee, dear Lord Christ, let me commend my soul to thee.

O heavenly Father, if I leave this body and depart this life, I am certain that I will be with thee for ever and ever, and that I can never, never tear myself out of thy hands.

So God loved the world that he gave his only-begotten Son, Jesus Christ, that whosoever believeth in him should not perish, but have eternal life.* [This text Luther repeated three times.]

Father, into thy hands I commend my spirit. Thou hast redeemed me, thou true God. Amen.

Martin Luther

* Jn 3:16.

The fear of temptation

It is an illusion to have too great a fear of combats. Never shrink from the occasions offered you by God of avoiding the danger of committing sin by avoiding the struggle.

Blush for your cowardice, and when you find yourself contradicted or humiliated say that now is the time to prove to your God the sincerity of your love. Put your trust in his goodness and the power of his grace.

And even should it happen that you occasionally commit some fault, the harm it will do you will be very easily repaired.

This harm, besides, is almost nothing compared to the great good that will accrue to your soul either by your effort to resist, or even by the humiliation these slight defects occasion you.

And if your temptations are altogether interior; if you fear to be carried away by your thoughts and ideas, get rid of that fear also.

Do not resist these interior temptations directly; let them fall and resist them indirectly by recollection and the thought of God.

And if you are not able to get rid of them in this way, endure them patiently.

Jean-Pierre de Caussade

Joy in God our Maker

Our Lord showed me our Lady, Saint Mary, to teach us this: that it was the wisdom and truth in her, when she beheld her Maker, that enabled her to know him as so great, so holy, so mighty, and so good. His greatness and his nobleness overwhelmed her. She saw herself so little and low, so simple and poor compared with God that she was filled with humility. And so from this humble state she was lifted up to grace and all manner of virtues, and stands above all.

This above all causes the soul to seem small in its own sight: to see and love its Maker. And this is what fills it with reverence and humility, and with generous love to our fellow-Christians.

The seeking, with faith, hope and love, pleases our Lord, and the finding pleases the soul and fills it with joy.

Julian of Norwich

The meaning of sanctification

At the same time that we are justified, yea, in that very moment, sanctification begins. In that instant we are born again, born from above, born of the Spirit: there is a *real* as well as a *relative* change. We are inwardly renewed by the power of God.

From the time of our being born again, the gradual work of sanctification takes place. We are enabled 'by the Spirit' to 'mortify the deeds of the body' of our evil nature; and as we are more and more dead to sin, we are more and more alive to God. We go on from grace to grace.

It is thus that we wait for entire sanctification; for a full salvation from all our sins – from pride, self-will, anger, unbelief; or, as the apostle expressed it, 'go on unto perfection'.

But what is perfection? The word has various senses. Here it means perfect love. It is love excluding sin; love filling the heart, taking up the whole capacity of the soul. It is love 'rejoicing evermore, praying without ceasing, in everything giving thanks'.

John Wesley

Do not despair

Do not fall into despair because of your stumblings.

I do not mean that you should not feel pain because of them, but that you should not consider them incurable.

For it is better to be wounded than to be dead.

There is indeed a healer: he who on the cross asked for mercy on those who were crucifying him, who pardoned murderers as he hung on the cross.

Christ came on behalf of sinners, to heal the broken-hearted and to bind up their wounds.

The Spirit of the Lord is upon me, he says; for that reason he has anointed me in order to proclaim good tidings to the poor. 'He has sent me to heal the broken-hearted, to proclaim deliverance to the captive, recovery of sight to the blind,'* and to strengthen the bruised by forgiveness.

And the Apostle says in his Letter, 'Jesus Christ came into the world to save sinners.'† And his Lord also testifies, 'I am not come to call the righteous, for they who are in good health have no need of a doctor; only those who are sick.'‡

Isaac of Syria

* Lk 4:18.   † 1 Tim 1:15.   ‡ Mk 2:17.

With pity, and not with blame

We know by the Faith that God took our nature upon him, and none but him; and furthermore, that Christ accomplished all the work necessary to salvation and none but him.

'I know well that you want to live gladly and joyfully for love of me, bearing all the trials that may come to you. But, since you do not live without sin, you are glad to suffer, for my love, all the tribulation and distress that may come to you. So let it be. But do not be too downcast by the sin that overtakes you against your will.'

I understood that the Lord looks on his servant with pity, and not with blame.

In God's sight we do not fall; in our sight we do not stand. As I see it both of these are true. But the deeper insight belongs to God.

Julian of Norwich

Pilgrimage

To go to Rome
Is much trouble, little profit.
The King whom thou seekest there,
Unless thou bring him with thee, thou wilt not
  find.

The Celtic Tradition

Loving continually

My soul is occupied
And all my substance in his service.
Now I guard no flock,
Nor have I any other employment,
My sole occupation is love.

Before the soul succeeded in
effecting this gift and surrender of
itself to the Beloved, it was
entangled in many useless occupations by which it
sought to please itself and others.

All this is over now, for all its thoughts, words and
actions are directed to God.

All my occupation now is the practice of the love of
God. All I do is done in love. All I suffer I suffer in
the sweetness of love. This is the meaning of David
when he says, 'I will keep my strength to Thee.'

John of the Cross

The dove

The little white dove
Has returned to the ark with
    the bough.
And now the turtle-dove
Its desired mate
On the green banks has found.

The Bridegroom calls the soul
the turtle-dove because when
it is seeking after the Beloved it is like the turtle-
dove when it cannot find its desired mate. It is said
that when it cannot find its mate it will not sit on
any green bough, or drink cool refreshing water, nor
rest in the shade, nor mingle with its companions.
But when it finds its mate it does all these things.

Such too must be the soul if it is to attain union with
the Bridegroom. The soul's love and anxiety must
be such that it cannot rest on the green boughs of
any joy, nor drink the waters of the world's honour
and glory, nor shelter in the shade of created help
and protection. It must mourn in its loneliness until
it finds the Bridegroom to its heart's content.

John of the Cross

Prayer of trust

O sweetest love of God, too little
    known,
he who has found thee is at rest.
Let everything change O my God,
that we may rest in thee.
Everywhere with thee O my God,
everywhere all things with thee
    as I wish.
O my God, all for thee, nothing
    for me.

Nothing for thee, everything for me.
All sweetness and delight for thee,
none for me.
All bitterness and trouble for me,
none for thee.
O my God, how sweet to me thy presence
who art the sovereign good!
I will draw near to thee in silence
and will uncover thy feet,
that it may please thee to unite me with thyself,
making my soul thy bride.
I will rejoice in nothing
till I am in thine arms.
O Lord, I beseech thee, leave me not for a moment
because I know not the value of my soul.

John of the Cross

On gentleness to ourselves

One form of gentleness we should practise is towards ourselves. We should never get irritable with ourselves because of our imperfections. It is reasonable to be displeased and sorry when we commit faults, but not fretful or spiteful to ourselves.

Some make the mistake of being angry because they have been angry, hurt because they have been hurt, vexed because they have been vexed. They think they are getting rid of anger, that the second remedies the first; actually, they are preparing the way for fresh anger on the first occasion.

Besides this, all irritation with ourselves tends to foster pride and springs from self-love, which is displeased at finding we are not perfect.

We should regard our faults with calm, collected and firm displeasure. We correct ourselves better by a quiet persevering repentance than by an irritated, hasty and passionate one.

When your heart has fallen raise it gently, humbling yourself before God, acknowledging your fault, but not surprised at your fall. Infirmity is infirm, weakness weak and frailty frail.

Francis de Sales

351

The spirit of prayer is for all times

The poverty of our fallen nature, the depraved workings of flesh and blood, the corrupt tempers of our polluted birth in this world do us no hurt so long as the spirit of prayer works contrary to them and longs for the first birth of the light and spirit of heaven.

All our natural evil ceases to be our own evil as soon as our will-spirit turns from it. It then changes its nature, loses all its poison and death, and only becomes our holy cross on which we happily die from self and this world into the Kingdom of heaven.

Reading is good, hearing is good, conversation and meditation are good; but they are only good at times and occasions.

But the spirit of prayer is for all times and all occasions. It is a lamp that is to be always burning, a light to be ever shining; everything calls for it, everything is to be done in it and governed by it, because it is and means and wills nothing else but the whole totality of the soul not doing this or that, but wholly, incessantly given up to God to be where and what and how he pleases.

William Law

The loss of hope

The loss of hope causes you more grief than any other trial. I can well understand this, for, as during your life you find yourself deprived of everything that could give you the least help, so you imagine that at the hour of your death you will be in a state of fearful destitution.

Allow me, with the help of God's grace, to set this trouble in its true light and so to cure you. What you want, my dear sister, is to find support and comfort in yourself and in your good works. Well, this is precisely what God does not wish and what he cannot endure in souls aspiring after perfection.

What! Lean upon yourself? Count on your works? Could self-love, pride and perversity have a more miserable fruit?

It is to deliver them from this that God makes all chosen souls pass through a fearful time of poverty, misery and nothingness.

He desires to destroy in them gradually all the help and confidence they derive from themselves so that he may be their sole support, their confidence, their hope, their only resource.

Jean-Pierre de Caussade

On exterior humility

Before we can receive the grace of God into our hearts they must be thoroughly empty of self-glory. Humility repulses Satan and preserves in us the gifts and graces of the Holy Spirit.

Noble birth, the favour of the great, popular esteem come either from our ancestors or from the opinion of others. Some are proud and conceited because they have a fine house, are well clothed, and cannot see how absurd this is. Some think proudly of accomplishment at music, knowledge of science or even personal beauty, but their glory in such things we call vainglory.

To know if a man is really wise, learned, generous, noble, observe whether his gifts make him humble, modest and submissive. If so, the gifts are genuine, but if they display themselves on the surface, they are less worthy.

Worldly honours are acceptable to him who receives them indifferently without resting in them or seeking them eagerly. They become dangerous and hurtful to him when he clings to and takes delight in them.

Francis de Sales

Love your neighbour

In the Gospel the Lord showed me clearly what his new commandment demands. I read in St Matthew: 'You have heard it said that you should love your neighbour and hate your enemy; but I say to you, love your enemies and  pray for those who persecute you' (Matthew 5:43–44).

We all have our natural likes and dislikes. We may feel more drawn to one person and may be tempted to go a long way round to avoid meeting another. Well, the Lord tells me that the latter is the one I must love and pray for, even though the manner shown me leads me to believe that the person does not care for me. 'If you love those that love you, what thanks are due to you? For sinners also love those who love them' (Luke 6:32).

Nor is it enough to love. We must prove our love. We take a natural delight in pleasing friends, but that is not love; even sinners do the same.

Thérèse of Lisieux

A catholic spirit

A man of a catholic spirit is one who gives his hand to all whose hearts are right with his heart: one who knows how to value, and praise God for, all the advantages he enjoys with regard to the knowledge of the things of God, the true scriptural manner of worshipping him and, above all, his union with a congregation fearing God and working righteousness: one who, retaining these blessings with the strictest care, keeping them as the apple of his eye, at the same time loves all, of whatever opinion or worship or congregation, who believe in the Lord Jesus Christ; who love God and man; who, rejoicing to please and fearing to offend God, are careful to abstain from evil and zealous of good works.

He is the man of a truly catholic spirit who bears all these continually upon his heart; who, having an unspeakable tenderness for their persons, and longing for their welfare, does not cease to commend them to God in prayer, as well as to plead their cause before men; who speaks comfortably to them and labours, by all his words, to strengthen their hands in God. He assists them to the uttermost of his power in all things, spiritual and temporal. He is ready 'to spend and be spent for them'; yea, to lay down his life for their sake.

John Wesley

It is so and it is well

In this love without beginning he made us, in the same love he protects us, and never allows us to be hurt in a way which would lessen our joy.

When judgement is given and we are all brought up above, then we shall see clearly in God the secrets now hidden from us.

In that day not one of us will want to say, 'Lord, if it had been done this way, it would have been well done.' But we shall all say with one voice, 'Lord, blessed may you be. For it is so, and it is well. And now we see truly that all things are done as it was ordained before anything was made.'

Julian of Norwich

On interior humility

St Thomas Aquinas tells us that the sure way of attaining to the love of God is to dwell on his mercies; the more we appreciate them, the more we shall love him.

Nothing can so humble us before the compassion of God as the abundance of his mercies; nothing so humbles us before his justice as the abundance of our misdeeds. Let us reflect upon all he has done for us, and all we have done against him. As we count over our sins in detail, so also we count his mercies.

We need not fear to be puffed up with knowledge of what he has done for us, if we keep before us the truth that whatsoever is good in us is not of us.

'What have you that you did not receive? And if you did receive it, why do you glory as if you had not received it?' (1 Corinthians 4:7).

A lively consciousness of mercies received makes us humble, for this knowledge gives birth to gratitude.

Sometimes we say we are nothing, weakness itself, but are ill pleased to be taken at our word. We pretend to take the lower place, but just to move up higher.

Francis de Sales

Christmas carol

This night is the long night,
It will snow and it will drift,
White snow there will be till day,
White moon there will be till morn,
This night is the eve of the Great Nativity,
This night is born Mary Virgin's Son,
This night is born Jesus, Son of the King of glory,
This night is born to us the root of our joy,
This night gleamed the sun of the mountains high,
This night gleamed sea and shore together,
This night was born Christ the King of greatness
Ere it was heard that the Glory was come,
Heard was the wave upon the strand,
Ere 'twas heard that his foot had reached the earth,
Heard was the song of the angels glorious,
This night is the long night.

The Celtic Tradition

Word made flesh

Let us weigh wisely, let
   us wonder at
   Wonders
      accomplished,
Nothing more
   wondrous in this
   world ever
      Will men's lips tell of,
God coming to us, he that created
   All of creation,
As God and as man, and God as a man,
   Equally gifted.
Tremendous, tiny, powerful, feeble,
   Cheeks fair of colour,
Wealthy and needy, Father and Brother,
   Maker of brothers,
This, sure, is Jesus, whom we should welcome
   As Lord of rulers,
Lofty and lowly, Emmanuel,
   Honey to think on.
An ox and an ass, the Lord of this world,
   A manger is his,
Bundle of hay instead of a cradle
   For our Lord of hosts.

The Celtic Tradition

A Christmas sermon*

Note how simply these events happen on earth, yet so highly regarded in heaven! There is the poor, young wife Mary, living in Nazareth, thought nothing of and regarded as one of the lowliest women in the town. No one is aware of the mighty wonder she is carrying. She herself keeps silent and says nothing, makes nothing of it, and thinks of herself as the lowliest woman in town. She sets off with Joseph her master . . . As they draw nigh to Bethlehem the evangelist presents them to us as the most wretched and disregarded of all the pilgrims, being forced to give way to everyone, till at last they are shown into a stable, and made to share shelter, table and bedroom with the beasts. While all this is going on, many a wicked man sits in the inn above and is treated like a lord. Not a soul notices, not a soul understands what God is doing in the stable. He leaves empty the palaces and stately homes, he leaves the masses to their eating and drinking and good cheer. Consequently, the comfort and treasure in Christ remain hidden from the likes of such people. O! what a thick, black darkness hung over Bethlehem that night, when she failed to apprehend so great a light within her walls! How decisively God shows that he has no regard for the world and its ways, what it is, what it has and what it does! How truly the world shows for its part that it has no regard for God, what he is, what he has, what he does . . .

Martin Luther

* Lk 2:1–14.

A Christmas thought*

To the Kingdom of Christ belong only poor, suffering men. It was for their sake that this King came down from heaven to earth. Therefore is his Kingdom a kingdom for hearts which are fearful, sorrowful and miserable. To such I now preach, just as the angel preached to the poor, frightened shepherds: 'Behold, I bring you good tidings of great joy!'

True enough, this great joy is offered to all people, yet it can be received only by those who have a troubled conscience and a grieving heart. The angel is saying, 'To those I have come, for such people is my message, to them my good tidings.'

Is it not a great miracle, that where the anxiety of conscience is greatest shall this joy be nearest; that where you are disheartened by fear and anxiety there shall come such sweet and abundant joy, that the human heart is too narrow to comprehend it? . . .

Listen to the angel's song, all you who have a troubled heart. 'I bring you good tidings of great joy!' Never let the thought cross your mind that Christ is angry with you! He did not come to condemn you. If you want to define Christ rightly, then pay heed to how the angel defines him, namely, 'A great joy!'

Martin Luther

* Lk 2:1–14.

St Ide's wish

'I will take nothing from my Lord,' said she, 'unless he gives me his Son from Heaven in the form of a baby to be nursed by me'. . . . So that Christ came to her in the form of a baby, and she said then:

'Little Jesus, who is nursed by me in my little hermitage – even a priest with store of wealth, all is false but little Jesus.

The nursing which I nurse in my house is not the nursing of any base churl, Jesus with the folk of heaven at my heart every single night.

Little young Jesus, my everlasting good, gives and is not remiss; the King who has power over all, not to pray to him will be repented.

It is Jesus, noble and angelic, not a paltry priest, who is nursed by me in my little hermitage; Jesus the son of the Jewess.

Sons of princes, sons of kings, though they come to my land, not from them do I expect any good, I prefer little Jesus.'

The Celtic Tradition

Speech and silence

The spiritual life is nothing else but the working of the spirit of God within us, and therefore our own silence must be a great part of our preparation for it, and much speaking or delight in it will be often no small hindrance of that good which we can only have from hearing what the spirit and voice of God speaks within us.

This is not enough known by religious persons; they rejoice in kindling a fire of their own, and delight too much in hearing of their own voice and so lose that inward unction from above which can alone newly create their hearts.

To speak with the tongues of men or angels on religious matters is a much less thing than to know how to stay the mind upon God, and abide with him in the closet of our hearts, observing, loving, adoring and obeying his holy power within us.

I have written very largely on the spiritual life, and he understands not my writings, nor the end of them, who does not see that their whole drift is to call all Christians to a God and Christ within them as the only possible life, light and power of all goodness they can ever have. I invite all people to the marriage of the Lamb, but no one to myself.

William Law

Love was his meaning

From the time that it was shown I desired often to know what was our Lord's meaning. And fifteen years after and more, I was answered in inward understanding, saying, 'Would you know your Lord's meaning in this? Learn it well. Love was his meaning. Who showed it you? Love. What did he show you? Love. Why did he show you? For love. Hold fast to this, and you shall learn and know more about love, but you will never need to know or understand about anything else for ever and ever.' Thus did I learn that love was our Lord's meaning.

And so I saw full surely that before ever God made us, he loved us. And this love was never quenched nor ever shall be. And in this love he has done all his works, and in this love he has made all things profitable to us, and in this love our life is everlasting. In our making we had beginning, but the love in which he made us was in him from without beginning, in which love we have our beginning.

Julian of Norwich

Holy desires grow by delays

God in his mercy looks on you not for what you are, nor for what you have been, but for what you wish to be.

St Gregory tells us that all holy desires grow by delays, and that if instead they die away, then in the first place they were never holy. For if a man feels ever less and less delight in new discoveries and in the unexpected resurgence of former desires, although he may have had a *natural* desire for what is good, *holy* it never was.

St Augustine says that the life of a Christian is nothing else but holy desire.

★   ★   ★

Farewell, spiritual friend, with God's blessing and mine! I pray Almighty God that true peace, wise counsel and spiritual comfort in God with abundance of grace, may be with you always and with all God's lovers upon earth. Amen.

Author of 'The Cloud of Unknowing'

Biographical Notes

All the books in the 'Enfolded in Love' series contain a substantial introduction telling of the life and work of their subjects. Brief biographical notes are given below.

ST AUGUSTINE was born in 354 at Thagaste in North Africa. He was baptized by Bishop Ambrose at Easter 386 and ordained priest in 391. Five years later he was consecrated Bishop of Hippo. His writings and sermons have exercised a deep influence on the Church. He died on 28 August 430. His feast day is 28 August.

JEAN-PIERRE DE CAUSSADE was born in Toulouse in 1675. He entered the Jesuit novitiate at the age of eighteen, and at thirty was ordained to the priesthood. He is best known for his treatise on *Abandonment to the Divine Providence* and his letters to the Sisters of the Visitation whom he directed. Latterly he suffered from increasing blindness, and died in 1751.

THE CLOUD OF UNKNOWING was written by an unknown author in the second half of the fourteenth century. It describes a 'work' or way of prayer to which a growing number are attracted today. The language indicates an East Midlands origin, and the author may have been a Cistercian hermit or Carthusian priest.

ST FRANCIS DE SALES was born in 1567 at the family château at Thorens near Annecy in France. He was ordained priest in 1593 and nine years later became Bishop of Geneva. His many books and letters have deeply influenced Christian spirituality. Over 2,000 of his letters may still be read. He died in 1622. His feast day is 24 January.

ST ISAAC OF SYRIA was born in the seventh century. He was for a short time Bishop of Nineveh before retiring to a monastic way of life. He is one of the greatest spiritual writers of the Christian East and his influence on the Orthodox Church continues to be profound.

ST JOHN OF THE CROSS was born at Fontiveros, Castile in Spain in 1542. He became a Carmelite at the age of twenty. In work and friendship he was closely associated with St Teresa of Avila. He is remembered today chiefly for his great mystical writings of which the best known are *The Ascent of Mount Carmel* and *The Dark Night of the Soul*. Early in his religious life he suffered much for the reforms in his Order which he saw were necessary. He died on 14 December 1591. His feast day is 14 December.

JULIAN OF NORWICH was born in 1342. On 8 May (and the following night) in 1373 she received sixteen 'showings' centred on the Holy Trinity and the Passion of Jesus. She wrote these down shortly after their occurrence and in a longer form, twenty years later, containing her meditations upon them. Her book, *The Revelations of Divine Love*, is regarded as a spiritual classic throughout the Christian world. For many years she was an anchoress in a cell attached to St Julian's Church in Norwich from which she probably took her name. The date of her death, perhaps about 1420, is not known. Her feast day is 8 May (Church of England Calendar).

MARGERY KEMPE was a contemporary of Julian of Norwich and has left an account of a visit to her early in the fifteenth century. She was born at Bishop's Lynn (now King's Lynn) in about 1373. She was the mother of fourteen children. Her many travels included visits to Rome and Jerusalem. Her book, now known as *The Book of Margery Kempe*, was dictated to a scribe, for she could neither read nor write. It was lost for many centuries but came to light in 1934. It makes fascinating reading in the modern Penguin Classics edition. She lived beyond the age of sixty, but the date of her death is not known.

WILLIAM LAW was born in 1686 in King's Cliffe in Northamptonshire. He was a non-juror (unable to swear allegiance to George I) and thus debarred from university or church appointments. He wrote many books of which the best known is *A Serious Call to a Devout and Holy Life*. Later he experienced what he called 'a second conversion', and what many regard as his best books (especially *The Spirit of Love* and *The Spirit of Prayer*) followed. He died in 1761. His feast day is 9 April (Church of England Calendar).

BROTHER LAWRENCE was born in Lorraine in eastern France in about 1611. He was converted at the age of eighteen, served for a while in the Army, retired wounded and permanently lame, and became a footman. Then he joined the Carmelite Order. For thirty years he was the monastery cook and later the cobbler. He is remembered for the record of his conversations and writings known as *The Practice of the Presence of God*. He died on 12 February 1691.

MARTIN LUTHER was born in Eisleben, Saxony on 10 November 1483. He was Professor of Theology in the University of Wittenberg in 1508 and then at Erfurt. He was excommunicated by the Pope in 1520 for what was regarded as his heretical teaching. He became a founder of the German Reformation, taking his stand on 'justification by faith in Christ alone'. His influence on the Church of England has been deep and lasting. He died in 1546.

ST TERESA OF AVILA was born on 28 March 1515. She entered the Carmelite convent of the Incarnation in Avila in 1536. Later she was to reform the Order, bringing a part of it back to the stricter primitive rule. The first house

of the reform was founded in 1562 and was followed by
fifteen more houses before her death on 4 October 1582.
Her writings have had a deep influence on Christian
spirituality. Her feast day is 15 October.

ST THÉRÈSE OF LISIEUX was born in the Normandy
town of Alençon in 1873. She became a Carmelite novice
at the unusually early age of fifteen. Later she became
Novice Mistress, but died after a long and painful illness,
borne with great fortitude, at the age of twenty-four. She
set out to teach her 'little way' described as 'the way of
trust and absolute self-surrender'. She was canonized by
Pope Pius XI on 17 May 1925. Her feast day is 1 October.

JOHN WESLEY, the son of an Anglican priest, was born
at Epworth, Lincolnshire on 17 June 1703. He was
ordained in the Church of England in 1728. In 1735 he
went as a missionary to Georgia, with his brother Charles.
He dates his conversion three years later, in London, on
24 May 1738. For over fifty years, until his death in 1791,
he preached the gospel throughout the country, travelling
on horseback perhaps a quarter of a million miles and
preaching over 40,000 sermons. He was the founder of
Methodism, which came to influence deeply the social life
of the country. His feast day (shared with Charles, brother
and hymn writer) is 24 May (Church of England
Calendar).

Index

The index below indicates the source books in the 'Enfolded in Love' series from which readings in this book have been taken.

373

Index

374